A Trauma-Informed Framework for Supporting Patrons

ALA Editions purchases fund advocacy, awareness, and accreditation programs for library professionals worldwide.

A Trauma-Informed Framework for Supporting Patrons

THE PLA WORKBOOK OF BEST PRACTICES

THE PUBLIC LIBRARY ASSOCIATION
SOCIAL WORKER TASK FORCE

CHICAGO | 2022

THE PUBLIC LIBRARY ASSOCIATION SOCIAL WORKER TASK FORCE develops and recommends a strategic and coordinated approach for PLA related to how public libraries address the social service needs of customers.

© 2022 by the American Library Association

Extensive effort has gone into ensuring the reliability of the information in this book; however, the publisher makes no warranty, express or implied, with respect to the material contained herein.

ISBNs
978-0-8389-4956-6 (paper)
978-0-8389-3820-1 (PDF)

Library of Congress Cataloging-in-Publication Data
Names: Public Library Association. Social Worker Task Force.
Title: A trauma-informed framework for supporting patrons : the PLA workbook of best practices / The Public Library Association Social Worker Task Force.
Description: Chicago : ALA Editions, 2022. | Series: ALA Editions special reports | Includes bibliographical references and index. | Summary: "This workbook provides a framework for what it means to use a trauma-informed lens and how to use that lens in interactions with library patrons. It offers various scenarios that will provide you the opportunity to integrate what you've learned so you can implement the trauma-informed framework in your work and offers a series of exercises that focus on self-care and self-assessment"—Provided by publisher.
Identifiers: LCCN 2021062239 (print) | LCCN 2021062240 (ebook) | ISBN 9780838949566 (paperback) | ISBN 9780838938201 (pdf)
Subjects: LCSH: Libraries and people with social disabilities—United States. | Libraries and people with social disabilities—United States—Problems, exercises, etc. | Psychic trauma.
Classification: LCC Z711.92.S6 T73 2022 (print) | LCC Z711.92.S6 (ebook) | DDC 027.6/63—dc23/eng/20220204
LC record available at https://lccn.loc.gov/2021062239
LC ebook record available at https://lccn.loc.gov/2021062240

Book design by Alejandra Diaz in the Laski Slab and Korolev typefaces.

♾ This paper meets the requirements of ANSI/NISO Z39.48-1992 (Permanence of Paper).

Printed in the United States of America
26 25 24 23 22   5 4 3 2 1

LEARNING ABOUT TRAUMA AND ADVERSITY can be uncomfortable. Trauma is widespread in our communities, and therefore it is likely that users of this workbook are survivors of their own traumatic experiences, in addition to witnesses of others' adversities. The authors have made efforts to construct this workbook through a trauma-informed lens. In order to ensure that this book is a valuable learning tool, examples of specific traumas and injustices will be discussed that may elicit strong reactions in readers. Please seek professional support when needed. This workbook is intended to increase curiosity and reflection on how public library work intersects with trauma and adversity in the community.

CONTENTS

Acknowledgments   *ix*
Introduction: No Easy Answers   *xi*

PART I	LAYING THE GROUNDWORK	1
Chapter 1	**What Is Trauma?**	3
Chapter 2	**Navigating Challenging Behavior**	11
Chapter 3	**Tools and Techniques**	15

PART II	STRATEGIES AND SCENARIOS	31
Scenario 1	**Mental Health Challenges**	33
Scenario 2	**Sleeping at the Library**	36
Scenario 3	**Strong Personal Odor**	39
Scenario 4	**Personal Belongings**	42
Scenario 5	**Suspected Intoxication, Under the Influence**	45
Scenario 6	**Substance Use**	48
Scenario 7	**Threatening Verbal and Nonverbal Behavior**	51
Scenario 8	**Unsheltered Teens**	54
Scenario 9	**Adult Self-Neglect**	57
Scenario 10	**Child Abuse or Assault**	60
Scenario 11	**Solicitation or Panhandling**	63
Scenario 12	**Stealing**	66
Scenario 13	**Child Unattended after Closing**	69

CONTENTS

PART III	PUTTING IT ALL TOGETHER	71
Exercise 1	**Now It Is Your Turn**	72
Exercise 2	**Begin Anyway**	73
Exercise 3	**Self-Care Assessment**	74
Exercise 4	**Self-Care Maintenance**	76
Exercise 5	**Emergency Self-Care Plan**	77
Exercise 6	**When Bad Things Happen**	78
Exercise 7	**Using Your Knowledge for Justice and Change**	79
Exercise 8	**Expand Your Knowledge**	80

Conclusion: The End Is Just the Beginning **81**
About the Principal Writer and Advisor and the Contributors **85**
Index **87**

ACKNOWLEDGMENTS

THE PUBLIC LIBRARY Association offers its deepest gratitude to the members of the PLA Social Worker Task Force (SWTF) and others whose hard work helped to make this book a reality. First and foremost, thank you to all of the contributors, and especially Debra Walsh Keane, cochair of the SWTF, who served as principal writer and advisor for this project. Thank you all for generously sharing not only your wisdom but also your passion for and commitment to this work. Last, but not least, this book would not have been possible without the support and dedication of Jamie Santoro, Senior Acquisitions Editor, ALA Editions. Thank you for your encouragement and guidance along the way.

INTRODUCTION
No Easy Answers

YOU MIGHT APPROACH this workbook with some apprehension. Maybe you've been working in a public library for years and are at your wits' end for how to handle challenging behaviors. Or you might be newer to the work and have heard "horror stories" about library staff getting yelled at or harmed by patrons. There is a lot of fear and uncertainty that can come with serving the public—after all, there are so many different kinds of people with so many different needs and behaviors! How can we possibly prepare for how to handle every situation?

Unfortunately, there are no easy answers. There isn't an "if X, then do Y and Z" formula that can guarantee you success every time. Every person you interact with at the library brings a richness of experience, identity, and personality that shapes who they are and how they exist in the world. There is no one-size-fits-all strategy to use when interacting with library patrons and coworkers.

But before you chuck this book across the room, please rest assured that it will provide a collection of powerful tools to add to your customer service toolbox. Though the topic of trauma can be heavy and emotionally draining, engaging with this material is ultimately a deeply hopeful act. In striving to learn more about challenging behaviors, we can come to see that people are complex and not simply "problems." Doing this work reinforces a belief that library staff can learn skills to be better. We are on a continual journey to become aware of trauma's impacts and to decrease harm. We will never be fully "trauma-informed," but we can increase our competence and ability to act in more skillful ways.

The goal of this workbook is to provide information and a framework for what it means to use a trauma-informed lens. In part I, "Laying the Groundwork," we provide a broader context for this work by discussing what trauma is and how it impacts library work. We offer a framework for how to utilize a trauma-informed lens in your interactions with library patrons. We introduce activities that invite you to reflect on common concerns you see at your library and the policies relating to those issues. In the "Tools and Techniques" chapter, we look at strategies for de-escalation and the impacts of involving law enforcement and banning patrons. In part II, "Strategies and Scenarios," we offer various scenarios that will give you the opportunity to integrate what you've learned and practice responding through a trauma-informed lens. Part III, "Putting It All Together," offers a series of exercises that focus on self-care and self-assessment.

You probably picked up this book because you've seen the impacts of trauma firsthand. At the library, we are uniquely situated among public institutions to interact with a diverse array of human beings. We welcome

INTRODUCTION

ACTIVITY 0.1 • KNOWLEDGE ENCAPSULATION

Use the chart below to encapsulate both your current knowledge on topics covered in this book and what you would like to know more about. After you have completed the book, come back and complete the last column, "What I Learned."

Topic	What I Know	What I Want to Know	What I Learned
Trauma			
Trauma-Informed Lens			
Behaviors as a Result of Trauma			
Library Policies			
Cultural and Historical Trauma			
Personal Biases			
Annoying Behavior			
Challenging Behavior			
Threatening Behavior			
Patrons with Mental Health Challenges			
Persons Sleeping at the Library			
Persons with Strong Personal Odor			
Persons with a Large Number of Belongings in the Library			

INTRODUCTION

Topic	What I Know	What I Want to Know	What I Learned
Possibly Intoxicated Patrons			
Substance Use at the Library			
Unsheltered Teens at the Library			
Adult Self-Neglect			
Child Abuse/Assault			
Panhandling			
Stealing			
De-Escalation			
Contacting Emergency Services			
Banning/Suspension			
Debriefing after an Incident			
Self-Care			

INTRODUCTION

everyone and encourage equal access to our resources. This means that we embrace individuals who have an incredible depth and breadth of life experience, in the knowledge that some of these life events may have been traumatic.

Trauma is not new. In the library and elsewhere, we have seen, heard, and felt the impacts that traumatic experiences have on individuals, families, and our communities for many years. Research is beginning to show that everyone is likely to be impacted by trauma, either through our own experiences or by interacting with others who have endured harm. By working alongside both coworkers and the public in the library, we are virtually guaranteed to work with people who have been traumatized. Trauma is considered a pervasive public health concern for this reason: It is all around us.

Yet we have all heard remarks such as, "Working in a library must be great! You just get to read books all day!" This is far from the truth: public library work increasingly means working with people. People who need the library for refuge in books. People who need a place to cool off or warm up and get water. Young people who need board books to help explain the death of a parent. People who need help with finding a job or applying for benefits. People who need information on systemic injustice so as to give language to their experiences of oppression. People who need resources on where to get food and shelter. People who need all this and so much more, with all of them looking to the library for help.

While we know that people who have experienced trauma use our library spaces, we also know that trauma can happen in the library itself. Our spaces are not immune to medical emergencies, violence, and even death. We also see the effects of others' traumas play out in front of us day after day and year after year through continued hardship and requests for help.

Bearing witness to these needs and traumas day in and day out can take its toll. Eventually, librarians may experience a profound shift in their worldview due to this exposure. We can develop symptoms like those of a stress disorder, including exhaustion and other physical ailments, behavior changes, and depression, anxiety, and feelings of hopelessness.[1] Library staff are not typically included in the list of those at risk for this trauma exposure, but we are not immune either.

What are library staff supposed to do when faced with such pervasive trauma? It can be overwhelming to consider the scope of adversity our communities face. We often do not feel equipped with the tools necessary to prevent or alleviate harm. It is crucial for us to take care of ourselves and understand that our work impacts our own well-being. Developing a robust self-care routine to cultivate your own personal wellness is one step. Seeking out supportive consultation and supervision around your work is another. Finding professionals, such as doctors, therapists, and peer counselors, who can help you process what you've gone through and ensure your own health and well-being is critical. In addition, finding opportunities for learning and reflection, such as this workbook, can help increase your understanding of how library work impacts you.

This work can be tough, but we believe it is valuable, worthwhile, and necessary. Ultimately, wanting to learn about trauma and improving our skills can generate hope for the future of this work and ourselves and other professionals. Thank you for joining us here.

NOTE

1. Françoise Mathieu, *The Compassion Fatigue Workbook: Creative Tools for Transforming Compassion Fatigue and Vicarious Traumatization* (New York: Routledge, 2012).

PART I

LAYING THE GROUNDWORK

CHAPTER 1

What Is Trauma?

TRAUMATIC EXPERIENCES ARE those that are emotionally or physically harmful, or even life-threatening. These experiences have lasting adverse effects on well-being and can impact an individual's mental, physical, social, emotional, or spiritual functioning.[1] Examples of trauma can include specific events, or a "timeline" trauma, like those that can be marked on a calendar: serious accidents, natural disasters, or the death of a loved one, to name a few. Trauma can also happen in an ongoing and repetitive manner through abuse and neglect or through continued experiences of racism, homophobia, and homelessness. Sometimes these traumas are referred to as "timeless" because they cannot be captured on a calendar as specific, one-time traumatic events might be. At a point somewhere between "timeless" and "timeline" traumas, our communities can experience a "time-limited" kind of trauma, where adversity and stress increase over a number of months and years in response to collective stressors, as with a pandemic. All kinds of traumas, both the singular event and the ongoing adversities, can have lasting effects on a person's sense of safety and trust and, as a consequence, can impact how they think, feel, and behave.

Generally, people are resilient. Many can survive adverse experiences without major changes to their worldview. However, trauma can affect anyone. It has no boundaries of age, income, gender, sexual orientation, race, ethnicity, or geography. Being human comes with the risk of adversity. Research suggests that anywhere between 55 and 90 percent of Americans have experienced at least one traumatic event.[2] In fact, it is estimated that 61 percent of adults have survived at least one of the several known "adverse childhood experiences" in their lifetime.[3] While no one is immune, some people and groups are more susceptible to traumatic experiences than others. For example, Black, Indigenous, and People of Color face race-based discrimination and oppression at much higher rates than white people. Women are more likely to face gender-based discrimination and violence than men, and trans and gender-diverse individuals are the ones most likely to be targeted for such abuse. The list continues for every known identity category. It is important to become familiar with the ways specific communities are exposed to ongoing trauma, while also understanding that every individual's experience is unique.

Trauma is also highly correlated with certain conditions and life experiences, including mental health conditions, substance use disorders, and homelessness. Again, this does not mean that every individual who lives with any of the above automatically experiences trauma; rather, the circumstances surrounding these conditions make it more likely that trauma may occur. Someone who is unhoused is much more likely to experience violence on the streets than someone who is housed. They are also more likely to experience both types of trauma—significant traumatic events like violence and ongoing adversities due to policies that target people who are homeless.

In order to survive and adjust to trauma, the human brain alters its functions. One way to think about this is the idea that trauma happens when "the rules" are broken. There are a number of "rules" that govern how people think about and feel safe in the world. Humans acquire these rules from infancy on, and together the rules establish a framework for understanding our experiences. Some of the rules related to trauma are seemingly simple, such as "the ground does not shake." Others are more abstract, like "people charged with protecting me don't hurt me." When these rules are broken during an earthquake or through abuse, our brains change to adapt to this new information.

Another example is the rule that "cars stop at stop signs." One of the authors of this workbook held deeply to this rule, until one day as a pedestrian she was struck by a car at a stop sign. The car did not stop where it was supposed to, and therefore the rule "cars stop at stop signs" was no longer true for her. Her brain—and importantly, her behavior—changed to incorporate the new information. "Cars stop at stop signs" was replaced with "cars do not stop at stop signs." Her new rule was designed to keep her safe. Following the accident, her brain was not interested in the nuance that most cars do stop at stop signs; what was most critical was that she didn't want to get hit again. Her brain, like all human brains, is wired for survival. So for years afterward, she had to make sure that each car had come to a complete stop at the stop sign before she could step into the street.

This same author has found that many drivers don't like what they perceive as her overly cautious behavior. Some will even shout at her, "Of course I was going to stop!" Yet standing on the street corner, she is uncertain that each car will stop because of the one that did not. When drivers shout at her, she wants to explain that her behavior is not an affront to their driving, but a perfectly logical response to a traumatic event she experienced decades earlier; however, the drivers usually speed away before she has the chance.

This example of a broken rule provides a simplified framework for how our thought and behavior can change in response to trauma. There is often a protective logic to behavioral responses to trauma, but like the drivers that speed away, library staff don't always have the opportunity to learn about how patrons' unusual behavior might be a learned adaptation. Very often, people who have experienced trauma are not able to explain the reasons behind their behaviors, as much of the underlying adaptation has occurred beyond their conscious awareness.

Apart from the way that trauma breaks the rules, it also changes brain chemistry. Experiences of trauma increase stress hormones, like cortisol, which can modify the brain's structure and functioning over time. To simplify a complex neurobiological process, the more cortisol that circulates in one's brain for a longer amount of time, the more likely one is to experience effects from these changes. When someone is exposed to trauma, they get a dose of cortisol sent to their brain. If the trauma cannot be resolved, or is persistent, as with ongoing adversity and timeless trauma, the brain does not have a chance to recalibrate and heal. Cortisol and harmful stress hormones stay heightened, which can result in serious health conditions and detrimental impacts on learning and development. It can also make emotional regulation more difficult or even impossible. Research shows that children who experience trauma at an early age and don't have help addressing it can face a number of health, mental health, and learning consequences across their lifetimes.[4] Unfortunately, experiences of trauma can accumulate over time, and if the brain does not recover, new learning may not be able to take place.

To return to the example of the car at the stop sign, our author has been able to adapt the "new" rule created by her trauma by incorporating more evidence that cars usually do, in fact, stop at stop signs. Her awareness continues to be heightened at intersections, but with practice and support, she is sometimes able to step off the curb before a car has fully come to a stop. For people who experience consistently high levels of stress, the brain is not provided with the opportunity to take in new information. Particularly with children, the new rules that trauma creates can become deeply ingrained, thereby making them challenging to change over time. This phenomenon can help explain why certain behaviors from childhood can persist; these behaviors might seem illogical to some, but they have merely become divorced from the original cause.

Dr. Nadine Burke Harris, a prominent researcher of childhood adversity, notes that "the difference between adaptive and maladaptive reactions is all about the when."[5] While in the heat of a traumatic experience, behavior kicks in that helps us to avoid harm or injury. When the threat is no longer present, the same behaviors may still kick in due to changes in the brain. This response can help explain why someone may have a heightened response to a library staff person that seemingly comes out of nowhere. For the person with a traumatic history, their behaviors are a continuation of a story that has become embedded in their brain and biology.

Experiences of trauma can put someone in a sustained state of hyper-arousal, where the brain is constantly on the lookout for danger. This means that a person will more quickly get into a "fight, flight, or freeze" response—reactions one typically has in response to a threat. Surviving trauma tends to attune the brain to potential threats, thereby helping one survive. Fight, flight, or freeze behaviors can be seen in library interactions. Someone may become argumentative, shout, throw things, or physically push people in response to what seems like a simple request; this may be a fight response based in a trauma history. Others might run (flight) away when confronted by library staff or other patrons. Finally, freeze behaviors mean that someone shuts down and is unable to respond to the situation. All three of these reactions can be confusing for library staff, given that they can appear extreme when compared to the trigger that initiated them. It is important to remember that the brain is trying to protect the trauma survivor, and fight, flight, and freeze are the ways it knows how.

The impact of trauma is not a choice, yet there is hope for recovery and growth after trauma. Human beings are resilient and can survive, and even thrive, in some incredibly harrowing situations. But the research indicates that people need support and connection to heal.[6] The aim of this workbook, then, is to provide library staff with tools and skills that can help reduce harm and promote healthy connections with others. Given the prevalence of traumatic experiences, the library is best served by using a trauma-informed lens to promote healthy environments and interactions for its patrons, employees, and community.

WHAT DOES IT MEAN TO BE TRAUMA-INFORMED?

Unfortunately, one can never be fully trauma-informed. There is no finish line or certificate of completion; rather, by applying a trauma-informed lens, library staff are able to use their knowledge of trauma and its impacts to inform how they create safety for patrons and staff. The first step to applying a trauma-informed lens is to cultivate an understanding of what trauma is, which the first part of this chapter has tried to do. This next section aims to lay out a framework that library staff can use to help guide their work to become more trauma-informed.

When faced with behaviors that seem incomprehensible, the question often comes up in exasperation: "What's wrong with you?" In applying a trauma-informed lens, "What's wrong with you?" gets reworked into "What happened to you?" The new question demonstrates an awareness that behavior can be shaped by trauma experiences and that a person is not bad or wrong.

The following is a framework adapted from sources on the basics and principles of trauma-informed care.[7] It provides five strategies for library staff to consider when applying a trauma-informed lens: Reflect, Protect, Connect, Respect, and Redirect. These strategies do not provide answers, but rather a way to integrate our knowledge about trauma, recognize when trauma responses might be occurring, respond in an appropriate manner, and take steps that help mitigate re-traumatization.

Reflect—Consider Cultural and Historical Issues

The public library, like many other institutions in the United States, has an institutional culture that is largely based on white middle-class norms. This means that the behaviors, speech patterns, and customs associated with whiteness are treated as the socially acceptable standard for behavior in the library as well. Divergence from this set of norms can result in disruption of library use, including banning someone from the library. When library staff assume that a rule or policy "goes without saying," they are unwittingly relying on and reinforcing this set of unspoken rules.

When applying a trauma-informed lens to library work, it is important to consider how the library itself has historically done harm to diverse individuals through exclusive policies and practices. Individually, library staff can reflect on and cultivate awareness about the cultural stereotypes and biases they hold: these can involve age, gender identity, sexual orientation, race, ethnicity, geography, housing status, or disability. Unwittingly acting on biases and stereotypes perpetuates harm; therefore, a level of awareness is critical.

In using a trauma-informed lens, the library strives to develop processes and protocols that are responsive to the needs of its diverse community members. This can be approached by recognizing the racial, ethnic, and cultural needs of the individuals served. Furthermore, recognizing and addressing experiences of historical trauma can be a crucial step in moving from reflection to action.[8]

This principle—reflect—is an ongoing process and will serve library staff well both in their individual patron interactions and with regard to the larger culture in which those interactions take place.

- What biases do I have? Check out Project Implicit for an opportunity to learn more.[9]
- How do these biases show up at the library?
- How has the library responded to different communities, including Black, Indigenous, and People of Color, people experiencing homelessness, and people with disabilities?

Protect—Promote Safety

Safety, both physical and psychological, is the cornerstone of a trauma-informed approach. Both staff and patrons require safety in the library to be able to thrive. Ensuring safety must be the highest consideration for everyone in library spaces. It is also important to explore what safety means for the patrons served. For example, though a police presence may suggest safety to some library users, others will view this presence as a threat. This is often particularly true for Black, Indigenous, and People of Color who have disproportionately endured a history of maltreatment by law enforcement.

What safety looks like can change depending on what is happening in a library. At baseline, safety can mean ensuring that spaces are clean, comfortable, and well-lit, and that interactions are courteous. If a situation arises wherein someone is aggressive, safety means maintaining an appropriate physical distance while using verbal de-escalation strategies. During a crisis, safety means working to ensure that no one is harmed or injured, which may involve clearing areas and relying on emergency services for assistance. Safety is key at all levels of escalation and stability, including after a crisis, when reestablishing both physical and psychological safety is needed. Professionals can be brought in to assist with debriefing and to provide information on coping with traumatic incidents. Questions to consider include:

- What trigger or stimulus could be contributing to this person's behavior?

- Are there basic needs, like food, water, and shelter, that may not be being met?
- Does this space promote physical safety? Where are the exits?
- How can I promote psychological safety?
- If a crisis is occurring, what is the "least amount of interaction necessary" for safety?[10]

Connect—Focus on Relationships

Healthy connection with others is one of the ways that people heal from adversity. Interpersonal trauma can cause survivors to experience interactions with others as threatening and unsafe. Library staff can work to establish consistent and friendly interactions with patrons that establish a baseline of safety. This can be done by welcoming patrons and sharing information about library services, in addition to staff explaining their role and sharing their names. Not every patron will want to engage with library staffers, and that is fine. Over time, by consistently providing space for trusting relationships, library staff can significantly impact someone's recovery.

It is important to remember that a power differential exists between staff and patrons, and this can serve as a reminder of trauma as well. Frustration and anger can be directed at library staff who represent the larger system of injustice at that moment; this is usually not a personal attack.

Building relationships with patrons can help send the message that they are important to the library community. Survivors of trauma often have internalized beliefs of being unworthy; by working to build relationships, library staff have incredible power to help restore someone's sense of value. Taking an extra moment to help a patron with their reference question can open up opportunities for further connection.

- Which patrons do I connect with most easily?
- Do I avoid engaging with certain patrons?
- What is my go-to method of initiating a conversation?
- How can I consistently provide friendly and accommodating service to people who do not want to engage?

Respect—Engage in Choice and Collaboration

Some patrons will have had their voices diminished by the library and the larger community. Respect is an important feature of any customer service model, and it is especially critical when working with a traumatized patron. People who have experienced trauma have often lost their decision-making capacities during and after a traumatic experience. Creating opportunities for shared decision-making invites a patron to regain some control over their library use experience. This helps counteract a top-down approach where leadership and authority demand certain behaviors and attitudes (which, unsurprisingly, can re-traumatize people).

Inviting feedback and participation when the library establishes its code of conduct and frames its policies and procedures for library use is one way to encourage collaboration. Empowering patrons to provide feedback with surveys and participatory action groups are ways to ensure that voices are heard. When setting up these groups and collecting feedback, it is important to pay attention to who is represented and who is missing from them. Many people who have been marginalized don't jump at the chance to participate in these exercises, as they have historically been excluded and not listened to. Library staff may have to make special efforts to include voices from all of their library patrons, particularly those who have not been able to participate in the past.

The library can foster trust in its community when people are treated with dignity, respect, and honesty. This means that participation and collaboration are ongoing, and that library users can count on consistency.

- How do I respect individual experience in the library?

- How do we promote collaboration?
- What feedback and participation does the library elicit from its patrons?
- What voices are missing? How can we create safety for those voices to be heard?
- How do we integrate the feedback we receive?

Redirect—Encourage Skill-Building and Confidence

Promoting self-determination is a critical way that library staff can support a trauma survivor's recovery. Many survivors are prevented from making decisions about their lives and are often told what they must do to receive services and treatment. Providing opportunities for choice and respecting the decision someone makes are crucial ways to promote self-determination.

During individual interactions with patrons, particularly if someone is escalated, providing choice can help that person regain a measure of control. There is a temptation to tell someone who is not following library policy that they need to leave immediately. First informing them of the policy, and then providing them with options for resolution, can help keep situations from escalating. For example, in a friendly way, let a customer know that the library has a shoe-wearing policy for health and safety. Give them a choice: they can put their shoes back on and stay; or if they want to keep their shoes off, they can do so, but they will need to leave the library. This allows the person to consider both options and decide what works best for them, without being told unequivocally what they must do.

Library staff can view each individual patron's strengths and respect their decision to make their own choices. It can be difficult to provide patrons with a list of resources for shelter only to find out that they chose to sleep on the streets. By respecting their decision, library staff honor the inherent abilities that the patrons have to keep themselves safe. Some trauma survivors have difficulty staying in a shelter environment due to their experiences with others; what is best for them in the moment may not resemble what an outsider might expect. Insisting that there is only one right way to solve a situation disempowers the survivor.

- How can I support a patron's decision-making?
- Does my library tell people what they must do?
- What opportunities exist for skill-building and confidence?
- How can I use a strengths-based approach to understand patrons' decisions?

THE ADVERSE CHILDHOOD EXPERIENCES STUDY

There is a growing understanding that trauma and adversity are not an "us versus them" issue, but an "all of us" issue. As you progress through this workbook, you may find that some of your own life experiences are being stirred up in your memory. It might be useful to review the questions in activity 1.1, which are from the Adverse Childhood Experiences (ACE) study questionnaire.[11] These are the questions that 17,000 participants in a 1998 landmark study answered—the results of which showed that more people had experienced trauma than previously imagined.

Of note is that the original participants in the ACE study were primarily white, college-educated, employed, and Kaiser insurance members. Given that the original participant pool lacked diversity, the questions themselves tend to overlook the adversity that often comes with existing outside of white, middle-class norms. As you work through these questions, you may be surprised that your own experiences are sometimes reflected in them. Others among us may find that our individual adversity or trauma experiences are not fully captured in the questions. The ACE questionnaire is not a perfect tool, but it helped launch a broader understanding and awareness of childhood adversity's pervasiveness. We offer it here for you to consider your own experiences with adversity.

CHAPTER 1 • WHAT IS TRAUMA?

ACTIVITY 1.1 • ACES QUESTIONNAIRE

Before your 18th birthday:

Did a parent or other adult in the household often or very often . . . swear at you, insult you, put you down, or humiliate you? Or act in a way that made you afraid that you might be physically hurt?	YES	NO
Did a parent or other adult in the household often or very often . . . push, grab, slap, or throw something at you? Or ever hit you so hard that you had marks or were injured?	YES	NO
Did an adult or person at least 5 years older than you ever . . . touch or fondle you or have you touch their body in a sexual way? Or attempt or actually have oral, anal, or vaginal intercourse with you?	YES	NO
Did you often or very often feel that . . . no one in your family loved you or thought you were important or special? Or that your family didn't look out for each other, feel close to each other, or support each other?	YES	NO
Did you often or very often feel that . . . you didn't have enough to eat, had to wear dirty clothes, and had no one to protect you? Or your parents were too drunk or high to take care of you, or take you to the doctor if you needed it?	YES	NO
Were your parents ever separated or divorced?	YES	NO
Was your mother or stepmother: Often or very often pushed, grabbed, slapped, or had something thrown at her? Or sometimes, often, or very often kicked, bitten, hit with a fist, or hit with something hard? Or ever repeatedly hit over at least a few minutes, or threatened with a gun or knife?	YES	NO
Did you live with anyone who was a problem drinker or alcoholic, or who used street drugs?	YES	NO
Was a household member depressed or mentally ill, or did a household member attempt suicide?	YES	NO
Did a household member go to prison?	YES	NO

If you answered "yes" to one or more of the above, you are like many of the people who answered these questions. A "yes" answer simply means that you are someone who has experienced trauma or adversity when you were young. The chances are that most of your colleagues and patrons could give a "yes" answer to one or more of these questions, too.

This questionnaire is not predictive of future illness or life experience, as it does not paint the whole picture of what it means to be human. The flip side of adversity is resilience and connection, which help mitigate the damaging effects of trauma on our brains and bodies. If you have concerns about your answers to the questions posed above, please connect with a trusted professional, doctor, therapist, or peer. Making sense of your own lived experience can help you find your bearings as you work with others.

NOTES

1. Substance Abuse and Mental Health Services Administration (SAMHSA), "Trauma and Violence," 2019, www.samhsa.gov/trauma-violence.
2. R. D. Fallot and M. Harris, *Creating Cultures of Trauma Informed Care (CCTIC): A Self-Assessment and Planning Protocol* (Community Connections, 2009), www.communityconnectionsdc.org/training-and-store/store#!/Creating-Cultures-of-Trauma-Informed-Care-CCTIC/p/80215860/category=22725096.
3. Centers for Disease Control and Prevention, "Adverse Childhood Experiences (ACEs): Preventing Early Trauma to Improve Adult Health," 2019, www.cdc.gov/vitalsigns/aces/.
4. Centers for Disease Control and Prevention, "Adverse Childhood Experiences (ACEs)," 2020, www.cdc.gov/violenceprevention/acestudy/index.html.
5. N. B. Harris, *The Deepest Well: Healing the Long-Term Effects of Childhood Adversity* (Boston: Houghton Mifflin Harcourt, 2018).
6. Harris, *The Deepest Well*.
7. Trauma Informed Care Project, "Essential Components of Trauma-Informed Judicial Practice," Orchard Place/Child Guidance Center, www.traumainformedcareproject.org/resources.php; Substance Abuse and Mental Health Services Administration (SAMHSA), "SAMHSA's Concept of Trauma and Guidance for a Trauma-Informed Approach," 2014, https://ncsacw.samhsa.gov/userfiles/files/SAMHSA_Trauma.pdf.
8. Project Implicit, "Project Implicit," 2011, https://implicit.harvard.edu/implicit/.
9. Project Implicit, "Project Implicit," 2011, https://implicit.harvard.edu/implicit/.
10. "Least Amount of Interaction," The Mandt System, September 21, 2014, www.mandtsystem.com/2014/09/21/least-amount-of-interaction.
11. Centers for Disease Control and Prevention "Adverse Childhood Experiences (ACEs)," 2020.

CHAPTER 2

Navigating Challenging Behavior

WHEN WE SEE disruptive behaviors at the library, we might automatically make assumptions or rely on stereotypes about why a situation is unfolding. Remember, it is possible that some of the difficult behaviors we observe are rooted in a patron's fight, flight, or freeze trauma response. In order to navigate patron behavior that may be considered challenging, it's important to consider a number of factors: how can you foster an environment in which patrons are successful? Setting patrons up for success includes limiting one's assumptions about *why* a behavior is happening and instead focusing on *what* is happening. Additionally, it can be helpful to connect with patrons before their behavior escalates. This can be accomplished by welcoming patrons to the library and referring to them by their names. Making such a personal connection is a worthwhile gesture to help generate rapport with patrons.

Keep in mind that some behaviors deemed challenging do not require a formal intervention. Ask yourself whether there is truly a problem at hand. There is a spectrum of behavior that extends from a challenge to an actual threat. Consider if the patron is merely posing an annoyance to you or if they are being a danger to themselves or to other patrons, library staff, or the library space. In the chart below (activity 2.1), you can list common challenging behaviors that you encounter at your library and where such instances fall on the continuum of challenging behaviors. What would be an appropriate response in each case? Consider whether children are involved and if the behavior requires the library to intervene as a mandated reporter (this varies by state). Even if you are not mandated, you are not barred from reporting; you are just not *required* to.

A LOOK AT LIBRARY POLICIES

Nearly every organization creates, adopts, and follows a set of policies to guide day-to-day operations, and libraries are no exception. Most people would be surprised to learn that their local library has policies in place to govern patron behavior and use, let alone that these policies are often quite lengthy. Paradoxically, at the same time there is a wide cultural stereotype among the public that satirizes what is essentially a library policy: "No Talking!" This phrase automatically conjures a stereotypical image of a librarian shushing someone, and this perception is one that librarians face on a regular basis. One reason why the "No Talking!" policy has taken hold in our popular concept of libraries is because to "not speak" is an unusual request: in very few other public places are people asked to regulate a natural human instinct like speaking to others. Though almost no libraries maintain an expectation of total silence, there remains a certain tension between

PART I • LAYING THE GROUNDWORK

ACTIVITY 2.1 • CONSIDERING PATRON BEHAVIOR

List five common behavior issues at your library and answer the following questions:

Issue	Is this an annoying behavior?	Is this a challenging behavior?	Is this a threatening behavior?	Is this a dangerous behavior?	What is the impact on other patrons, library space, and staff?

maintaining a quiet study space and the reality that people will, and need to, speak.

Furthermore, when human behavior is regulated by someone with authority, like a library staff person, there is an overwhelming chance that unconscious biases will impact for whom and how these policy enforcement requests are made. This disparity is simply a fact of being alive; no one is without biases against or preferences for certain groups of people. What library systems need to be mindful of is when their policies unwittingly target specific patrons or groups of patrons unfairly. This can happen in several ways, either by setting impossible standards (like a silent children's area), or in a discrepancy between who is asked to comply with these standards and who "gets a pass." Children of color will often experience over-regulation of their behaviors in libraries, whereas white children may be allowed to yell and engage in play according to their stage of development and culture.[1]

As we begin to inspect the policies our libraries have, there can be many big questions and painful realities to address, such as a history of racism, ableism, and bigotry ingrained in the adoption of predominantly white, middle-class norms. And when policies are lengthy and wrapped up in legalese and verbose language, we must be able to pare each policy down to its roots. Answering the question "What is the reason for this policy?" can be a complex task. But getting to the heart of the policies that we enforce can help us understand why we make the requests that we do, and why we ask our patrons to comply with those requests. If we cannot come up with solid reasons (grounded in equity) for why a policy is reasonable, it might mean that the policy is perpetuating harm, and not ensuring safety.

Activity 2.2 is a matrix of questions that you can use to help you practice dissecting your library's policies.

The policies a library has reflect the values it holds as an organization. If the policies are not expressly linked to a library's mission, vision, and values, then their subtext will set the tone for what the library's values really are. If many of a library's policies are geared to ensuring that the library is used in a "correct" and limited way, it is very likely that entire demographics and groups of people are being excluded. This is because the subtext of the policies is saying, "This kind of library user doesn't belong here."

Ultimately, any effective library policy should accomplish one or both of these goals: decreasing risk and increasing access to library resources. Decreasing risk concerns the way we promote both physical and psychological safety in a public place. Safety, in turn, is linked to our access goal: dangerous behaviors can fundamentally disrupt the public's ability to safely use library resources. The entire point of a public library is to ensure that as many people as possible can use the resources the library offers. Ensuring access can range from maintaining long hours of operation, to promoting computer use at computer stations, to providing high-quality reference interviews. Moreover, we want our libraries to act as places of refuge for our community members. As you consider the implications of your library policies, you should take an expansive view of library resources beyond materials and technology to include space, access to water and restroom facilities, and a place to rest. This view can help ensure equity of access for all library users and community members.

NOTE

1. E. Barnett, "People of Color, Especially Children, Most Likely to Be Asked to Leave Seattle Libraries," *South Seattle Emerald*, August 22, 2018, https://southseattleemerald.com/2018/08/22/people-of-color-especially-children-most-likely-to-be-asked-to-leave-seattle-libraries/.

ACTIVITY 2.2 • LIBRARY POLICIES REVIEW

List three policies that govern behavior (for example, fines, unattended children, sleeping, etc.). Answer the questions that follow.

Policy #1:	
What is the reason for this policy?	
What are the desired outcomes of this policy?	
How is this policy implemented?	
What does the data about this policy reveal?	
Have impacted communities been engaged in the process of developing this policy?	
Who benefits from or is burdened by the policy?	
How might the policy be made more equitable?	

Policy #2:	
What is the reason for this policy?	
What are the desired outcomes of this policy?	
How is this policy implemented?	
What does the data about this policy reveal?	
Have impacted communities been engaged in the process of developing this policy?	
Who benefits from or is burdened by the policy?	
How might the policy be made more equitable?	

Policy #3:	
What is the reason for this policy?	
What are the desired outcomes of this policy?	
How is this policy implemented?	
What does the data about this policy reveal?	
Have impacted communities been engaged in the process of developing this policy?	
Who benefits from or is burdened by the policy?	
How might the policy be made more equitable?	

CHAPTER 3

Tools and Techniques

ALONG WITH THE trauma-informed framework presented in the previous chapter, there are several tools and strategies that library systems can use in a trauma-informed way to help support both library operations and their patrons. In our daily interactions with patrons through reference interviews and resource questions, library staff can use trauma-informed approaches and best practices that can help every interaction go more smoothly. When we encounter an upset patron, there are ways we can approach de-escalation that can help mitigate trauma reactions. There are weighty questions about how and when to involve police and emergency responders at our libraries; trauma-informed principles can help guide our practices in these areas to ensure equitable care and to decrease the risk of traumatizing and re-traumatizing our patrons, our staff, and our communities. Taking away a patron's right to use the library, through suspensions, bans, and trespasses, is rife with the potential to activate trauma responses for individual patrons while also denying them needed services; these actions cannot be taken lightly by library staff. Ultimately, given that all of this work can be so difficult and emotional, there is also a need for library staff to come together and create psychological safety around their work through debriefing. This work is challenging, and the debriefing process is challenging as well; some debriefing can be done through a standard supervisory process or relationship within the library context, but there may be times when bringing in trained professionals is required. There is a lot to think about when applying trauma-informed principles to a library's day-to-day functioning, so let's start with the most typical interaction: providing patrons with information about social service resources.

RESOURCE NAVIGATION, REFERRAL, AND THE REFERENCE INTERVIEW

A primary task for library social workers is assisting with resource navigation and referrals; though some assessments and recommendations require social services expertise, there are simpler referrals that other library staff members are capable of fulfilling equally well. Librarians are often aware of the social service resources in the locality, and are able to provide quick referrals to patrons without needing to consult a library social worker. Similar to the reference interview, librarians can ask specific questions regarding what type of assistance the patron is seeking, in order to best serve them. When a patron comes to us with a question, we can respond in a human-centered way by taking a few extra moments to share in the importance of their question, about social services or any other library resource. It is important that we assist when we can because being handed a list or being directed to a website can cause a negative reaction for someone who has had trouble navigating services in the past. This section will provide librarians with tools to assess patrons' needs and make effective resource referrals, which may include involving the library social worker in complex situations. Additionally, boundaries and limitations will be examined, as we want to ensure that librarians work within their scope and thus avoid becoming overloaded.

Reference Interview Questions

Asking questions is essential to assessing a patron's needs. In the social work profession, assessment (whether formal or informal) is the first task when meeting with a new client. Similarly, librarians—particularly reference librarians—begin their interactions with assessment. The following list of sample questions can be used as a guide for social service-related resource navigation.

- How can I be most helpful to you?
- Is there an immediate need I can help you address?
- Tell me a bit about what you're looking for.
- Are you familiar with ____? (could be a resource or an organization)
- Do you have a place to stay tonight? Is it safe?
- When was the last time you had something to eat?
- Preferences and/or needs to consider:
  - Resources in a preferred language
  - Resources for a specific ethnic or cultural group
  - Gender-specific resources
  - Resources that are or are not religiously affiliated
  - Resources that are ADA-compliant
- What else might you need to follow through on this?
- Can you think of anything that might get in the way of ____ (Accomplishing this? Getting to the appointment on time? Making that phone call?)
- Sounds like there are several things you want to address. What is most important for you today?

Open-Ended Questions

Open-ended questions are meant to gather information. They cannot be answered with one word, such as "yes" or "no." Open-ended questions invite a free-form response and may lead your conversation in an unexpected and valuable direction. We suggest asking more open-ended questions than closed-ended questions.

- Start with questions about who, what, where, when, or how.
- Avoid asking "why." This could be interpreted as judgmental or feel like an interrogation.
- Tell me about...
- What have you already tried?
- Who else have you gone to for assistance?
- What is your biggest concern today that you'd like to address?
- What is your preferred geographic area?
- When did you first start working on this?
- How can we ____ (Work together to solve this problem? Make sure you get to that appointment?)

RESOURCES: WHERE TO SEARCH

If you don't have a social worker on-site or a resource guide readily available, don't fret. Your city or county government probably has databases, lists, and professionals available to assist you. You can also create an internal resources list that is tailored to your location and library system. It is important to understand that each provider organization will provide only a limited number of services or have a specialty. For this reason, it may be necessary to make multiple referrals to address all of a patron's needs. Listed below are several potential information sources you can consult when working with patrons.

ACTIVITY 3.1 • IDENTIFYING RESOURCE GAPS

List **5–10** social service resources available in your area, identify three gaps in these resources, and commit to doing some research to find resources that can fill those gaps.

What resources does your library use to assist patrons with social service needs?

1	
2	
3	
4	
5	
6	
7	
8	
9	
10	

Where are there gaps in the resources?

Do some research in your community to find resources to fill in those gaps. List the new resources below.

Local Resource Guides

Many library systems create and maintain local resource lists. These may be designed for staff only or to be printed and shared with patrons. Any staff member(s) can create a list. This is a great task for a librarian or an intern wanting to learn more about their local community resource landscape, or even a group of staffers. Most important is identifying a point person who will keep the list updated, as resources and information change often. We suggest organizing the list by type of need (food, shelter, medical providers, showers, etc.) and including only basic information like location and phone number. If the list includes details like hours of operation or criteria to access, it will require constant updating. You should always call, or suggest that a patron call, an organization to confirm the hours and type of services it provides before sending a patron there.

City Government Websites and Staff

Though each community is different, most local government institutions and organizations are aware of the social service resources that are available in their jurisdiction. Many city websites include Social or Human Services Department pages or lists of provider agencies and resources. You can also contact your city's Human and Social Services Department staff directly for recommendations. Additionally, having a contact person in the city government is valuable to the library for many reasons. If a government aid office does not provide the specific resource you are looking for, they will likely be able to make referrals to partner organizations.

County Websites

In addition to city websites, county websites often list social service organizations and resources. If your library is located in a large county, you may need to narrow your search by region. Utilizing a county website can be particularly helpful if you are assisting a patron in a neighboring county—perhaps they are relocating and want to know what is available in their new area.

Resource Databases

Sometimes it can be helpful to reach out to a local community-based organization, such as a homeless shelter or food pantry, to ask if they have a resource database or guide that they refer to when providing services to their clients. As previously mentioned, each organization provides only a limited number of services, making it necessary to connect with multiple resources to address all of a patron's needs. Furthermore, community-based organizations tend to have relationships with each other to fulfill their goals of community-building and cohesion.

Crisis Lines and Websites

Most national and local crisis lines have websites. The website will likely include information about resources connected to their services and service population. Their services may include a noncrisis line staffed with people to provide support and resource navigation assistance.

Chambers of Commerce

Chambers of Commerce have updated information and contact persons for local businesses and nonprofits. This aligns with their goal to provide information about the community to its residents and visitors. Chamber of Commerce staff and websites are an effective resource for any and all kinds of services—legal, medical, employment, residential, tourism, transportation, and so on.

SEARCH TIPS

Regardless of what search tool you are using, these resource navigation tips will help you make effective referrals.

- *Always contact a resource* to verify their hours of operation, availability, and procedures before sending a patron there. Social

services are constantly changing, so it is important to call even if your resource list was recently updated. You want to make sure that patrons are successfully able to access services rather than hitting dead ends, which can cause frustration and cause patrons to give up.
- *Clarify* what the patron will need to access services. Some organizations have no requirements to access their services, but the majority require identification, an address, and contact information. A state ID or driver's license is preferred, but temporary or other forms of ID are generally accepted as well. If someone is experiencing homelessness, organizations usually have a protocol for those without a permanent address or contact information. Government aid offices may require more documentation than social service agencies. For example, if a patron needs to apply for food benefits, they will be asked to prove their identity and income. If a patron does not have identification, your focus may shift to helping them obtain the necessary documentation.
- *Inquire about additional considerations*, such as building accessibility, language translation services, or pet-friendly facilities. You will have gathered information about the patron's specific needs from the reference interview or assessment.
- *Troubleshoot any barriers* to accessing the resource. For example, you might need to look up a bus route or provide a bus ticket for the patron to physically get to the referral site. Other barriers can include limited access to childcare or lack of clean or professional clothes for employment purposes. Try to address these barriers with additional resources as needed.
- *Prioritize* when a patron has multiple needs. Most of us have encountered a patron with a long, urgent list of things they need help with. These needs may be outside the scope of librarian work and capacity. In these situations, it could be appropriate to refer the patron to a library or community social worker. However, prioritizing needs can still be helpful when a patron comes to you with a lot of requests. The patron's access to basic needs such as food and shelter is considered more of an immediate need than getting a state ID, so asking the patron questions about their basic needs is a great place to start. Sample questions regarding basic needs are: "Do you have a place to stay tonight?"; "When was the last time you had something to eat?"; and "Do you feel safe at home?" If someone's basic needs are being met, helpful statements for their assessing priorities are: "What is the most important thing to address today?" or "You can pick one thing to do today and come back tomorrow for the next."

EFFECTIVE DE-ESCALATION IN A TRAUMA-INFORMED ENVIRONMENT

Often, the work we do to create trauma-informed environments and have trauma-informed interactions can set the stage for effective de-escalation. We all want the magic word or phrase to say in a heated moment with a patron that will diffuse the tension immediately. But, as we've seen with our trauma-informed principles, we approach de-escalation with a toolbox approach rather than a guaranteed one-size-fits-all strategy. The principles we have explored so far will serve us well in thinking about de-escalation techniques. The goal of our library work, ultimately, is to provide library service to as many people as we can safely. And so the goal of our de-escalation work is to keep people in the library, as opposed to kicking them out or having them removed.

Pre-Escalation

When we arrive at the need for de-escalation, it can mean that many of our trauma-informed strategies have not been deployed effectively. Many skills labeled "de-escalation" are actually used to keep a situation from escalating into a crisis in the first place. The fundamental concept in our de-escalation philosophy is that most of the skills we can use occur before a situation becomes heightened. Trying to create trauma-informed libraries and practicing the strategies outlined in this workbook can lay the foundation for the work that happens before escalation occurs. Our term for the work in this de-escalation context is "pre-escalation"; that is, everything we do to try to prevent an issue from becoming a crisis in the first place. And the great news is that this "pre-escalation" work can prevent most issues from requiring higher levels of intervention. Welcoming patrons, building relationships with them, and consistently providing friendly service are key here. Patrons develop trust in us and our services when we provide experiences that promote respect and dignity over time.

Escalation can occur because of misunderstandings. When we work in the library, we can become very accustomed to our rules, regulations, and policies because we think about and enforce them every day. It can become hard for us to believe that someone would not know what behaviors we expect of them. But, as we have discussed, policies are often not front-of-mind for our patrons, and they are based on norms that do not ring true for everyone. This means that conflict can arise when we see a patron breaking a rule in our codes of conduct.

Kindly Inform, and Enforce through Choice

To help de-escalate these misunderstandings, it is useful to kindly inform our patrons of the behavior expectations that we have in our libraries. This is where knowing the reason why a policy is in place can be very helpful. Let's use the requirement that patrons must wear shoes in the library as an example.

Kindly Inform

"We're glad you're here! We ask that everyone in the library wear shoes for health and safety." Once a patron is aware of this behavior expectation, a trauma-informed approach to the conversation is to enforce the policy by providing them with a choice.

Enforce through Choice

"If you'd like to stay in the library, we will need you to wear your shoes." By framing it this way, we are offering a decision, as opposed to telling the person that they must follow our mandate. If they prefer to keep their shoes off, they are welcome to do so outside of our library. As we have discussed, people who have experienced trauma have had their decision-making abilities taken from them. Providing choice can help keep someone from feeling trapped or like they are being yelled at—both experiences that can escalate any of us. When we ask for any of our policies to be followed, there is usually always a choice to be made: you can change your behavior to be safer and stay in the library, or you can choose to leave. This helps someone preserve their autonomy. (More rarely, someone may choose both not to leave and not to change their behavior; we will discuss responses to this in the "Emergency Services" section later in this chapter.)

NONVERBALS

Our nonverbal presentation, which involves eye contact, smiling, and where and how we position our bodies, is an important part of both our pre- and de-escalation strategies. Although "appropriate" eye contact varies across cultures and personal experience, we know that many people experience direct, intense eye contact as aggressive and escalating. Similarly, smiling can be a wonderful tool to help create a welcoming and warm environment; in a heated interaction, though, a smile can be interpreted as condescending and belittling.

Some people who have experienced trauma have not had control over how their bodies were treated; people in positions of power, which includes us as library employees, want to be mindful of how we use our own bodies in response to others. The feeling of being towered over by a much larger person is not a comfortable one. So whether that is a library staff person looming large over a patron, or a patron standing tall over us, maintaining distance between ourselves and an upset person is useful in a number of ways. It allows us to keep ourselves safe by keeping out of range of a patron's limbs, and it also expands our visual range; being able to see someone's whole body (hands and feet) allows us to better assess any potential dangers. It also simultaneously creates space for an upset patron to feel like they have room to breathe and that they will not be cornered or trapped. Recommendations for the "right" amount of space in de-escalation vary between 1.5 to 3 feet, or up to two arm's lengths. You should consider practicing different distances with coworkers to see what works in your space.

VERBALS

How we speak can be as important in de-escalating someone as what we say. Tone is very important, because condescension, annoyance, and sarcasm can quickly escalate someone who might already be confused or frustrated. Try to speak clearly and at a speed that promotes understanding. This will be different for everyone, so developing an awareness of our own typical speech style and how it can be interpreted by others is a useful place to start. When we are invited to speak slower, louder, or make any other change, keep in mind that the goal is to work together with the patron to communicate effectively. In general, speaking slowly and at a moderate volume are useful in de-escalation. Modeling the manner of speech we hope to see from our patrons in heated moments can help set the tone for the interaction and can eventually help someone de-escalate on their own—it's rare that someone who is being yelled at will calm down.

What we say in a heated moment is also very important. We want to be aware of commanding and demanding language. "You have to do this!" or "Calm down now!" are quick ways to escalate someone, which is the opposite of what we are going for. Taking a moment to acknowledge what the patron's experience is (or might be) can help take the edge off a confrontation. Saying "I can see that you're frustrated" or "This was not what you were hoping for when you came here today" signals that we are aware of the feelings that might be contributing to someone's upset state. Acknowledging the patron's feelings in a genuine way can help them feel that their concerns are understood and valid. (Activity 3.2 can help you transform certain statements into ones that reflect trauma-informed principles.)

EMERGENCY SERVICES

It can be hard to know when to call 911 to help respond to a situation at the library. It's important to consider the scope of the library staff's role when wondering whether to make a call. We know that library staff are information specialists and are particularly skilled at research, technology, community programming, and interacting with the public seeking these services. Library staff are also able to help guide their patrons to appropriate behaviors that comply with their code of conduct, both by encouraging trauma-informed environments and by using de-escalation skills. Depending on your library's practices, you may also be able to provide basic first aid while waiting for emergency responders to arrive. What library staff are not able (or expected!) to do includes providing medical care, responding to emergencies of life and health, or taking action on illegal activities. These would be instances when calling emergency services are necessary.

Some library staff have expressed increased concern about calling the police for fear that a patron may be mistreated, harmed, or even killed by officers. In the United States these concerns have taken on particular urgency recently, and many states and municipalities are now looking into alternatives to policing to help decrease this risk. While there will be emergencies for which police are the only appropriate resource, it is important that we are aware of all of our response options in our geographic area. Many

PART I • LAYING THE GROUNDWORK

ACTIVITY 3.2 • IN OTHER WORDS

List below some common statements that you or your colleagues often make at the library. Using a trauma-informed lens, transform the statement into a more person-centered one. The first two statements in the table are examples.

Instead of saying:	Say it in a way that reflects trauma-informed principles:
It's our policy.	Here's how I can help you . . .
There is no sleeping in the library.	I noticed you're having trouble staying awake. Is everything okay?

Word Choice Matters

Using stigmatizing, dehumanizing language can impede our efforts to assist library patrons. Language is constantly evolving. The options presented in this section are currently in use, but may change. Try to stay up-to-date on language choices.

Think about why you are "labeling" patrons in the first place. Describing other human beings is a controversial business, and involves power dynamics. We want to be as objective, neutral, and standard as we can. Try to be thoughtful about the labels you use.

Noting that a patron "presents as" or "appears to be" this or that acknowledges that we don't know how someone identifies, and that the report is based on our observation. Use "they" as a neutral pronoun or when unsure. Best practice—be as respectful as possible!

Get These Words Circulating in Your Library
- Unhoused Person; Patron Experiencing Homelessness (instead of Homeless Person, Transient)
- People without Housing (instead of the Homeless)
- Describe relevant behaviors instead of labeling; for example: Person who appears to be talking to themselves and/or hearing voices (instead of Crazy, Nutcase, Mental, Retarded)
- Person who uses drugs; Person who injects drugs (instead of Drug Addict)
- Person who may be intoxicated (instead of Alcoholic, or Drunk)

Race
- Use: white, black, brown; person of color; Latinx, Asian, African American, Indigenous.

Gender
- Use: male, female, nonbinary, or gender-diverse.

Age
- Guess by decade – 20s, 30s, 40s, and so on

communities are considering having social workers and counselors who can be deployed to respond to someone having a mental health crisis, as opposed to sending officers. Elsewhere, some police forces have officers with special training so as to be better able to respond to mental health emergencies; for example, there are crisis intervention teams (CITs) or other programs where clinicians co-respond with police officers. You should consider connecting with both your local mental health center and local law enforcement to discuss what options are available for urgent and emergency responses. Becoming knowledgeable about who responds to which calls can help library staff know who to contact in the moment.

There is a balance to be struck when contacting emergency services. Along with knowing who to call, knowing when to call is key. Every situation is going to be different, but for those that are not life- or health-threatening emergencies or don't involve violence or weapons, library staff are acting within their scope to try and resolve disputes or other issues. The main tool library staff have will be to use communication—and doing this effectively can de-escalate most situations! But when words and other de-escalation tools do not (or would not) work, this is when staff can use their other main tool: bringing in the appropriate responders. We want to be clear and consistent in our procedures for the use of this tool, as bias in policing reflects the unconscious biases that many of us hold. Consider whether we would have the same response if an escalated patron presented as white, black, or brown; disabled or able-bodied; or disheveled or well-dressed. We know that communities of color are more likely to view police as threats, as opposed to helpers. One way to mitigate the concerns we may have about policing is to be very clear on what situations library staff can handle, and when we must rely on emergency services. Instead of over-policing, our aim is "appropriate policing"—using our skills to take care of most issues, and calling 911 only in the emergencies when it's needed.

SUSPENDING LIBRARY PRIVILEGES

Given how valuable our library services can be—access to information and technology, in addition to respite from weather and access to drinking water and restroom facilities—restricting a patron's library use is not a decision to be taken lightly. When your library (or library system) decides that a person's behavior is not safe for the library, it may prevent that patron from returning to the library for a set amount of time, or suspend their library privileges. Bans and suspensions are imposed by the library based on policies (like the code of conduct) that are often approved by the library board of trustees. From a trauma-informed point of view, these processes are difficult. We want to view people as distinct from their behavior, and this is where the idea of suspending someone's library privileges can fit more easily into our framework than banning someone outright from the library. Your library may use the terms *ban* or *suspension* interchangeably; while they are effectively the same, a semantic difference exists between them. When a library uses the word *banning* to describe restricting a patron's privileges it suggests that the person is "bad" or "wrong." Using *suspension* or *suspension of privileges* can help both staff and patrons see that it is someone's behavior that is unacceptable, as opposed to the person themselves. Your library will want to inspect its processes for restricting library use privileges, as this is another area where library work can be fraught with bias. Consider whether there are automatic suspensions for set lengths of time for specific behaviors. Are these equitable across different life circumstances? What would cause the library to ban a person for life? In most cases, when someone's behavior is safer and various reinstatement procedures have been met, they will be welcomed back to the library.

How we inform a patron that their library privileges have been suspended can have a big impact on their ability to return. We have seen processes that range from giving the patron a card in a bright color that says "You are BANNED!" to lengthy letters that detail every infraction a patron is reported to have committed. Both of these approaches send similar messages: "You are not welcome here." What is most useful is communication that is brief, understandable, and clear. Outlining how someone can go about resolving their suspension is often what is most useful, and reviewing your library's behavior expectations can often be most easily done through conversation with them.

A low-barrier reinstatement process is important as well. If the process for someone to come back to the library involves a conversation with a manager, security staff member, or social worker, be mindful of how easily the patron can access those meetings. Barriers like phone access, transportation, and the available times of these meetings can unwittingly result in a lifetime suspension if a patron is unable to find workarounds. Some systems have drop-in availability for resolution meetings, so as to welcome back patrons who may have difficulty keeping a scheduled appointment. Suspending a child or youth can be even more complicated: if a child has their privileges revoked, and the resolution includes a parent or guardian keeping a meeting with library staff during their work hours, the child may be set up for a de facto lifetime ban. This denies the child a safe place to be and access to crucial social and literacy experiences. Consider what alternatives may be available to your library; a few libraries are considering doing away with suspending children for this very reason and implementing a restorative justice approach for reinstatement.

When welcoming a patron back to the library, you should plan to set clear expectations that are behavior-focused. Consistency is key. We know that people who have experienced trauma can recover when they have structure and know what to expect. Surprises and "Gotchas!" can trigger trauma-survival responses, which can look like the very behaviors that caused a suspension in the first place. Framing the reinstatement of privileges as an opportunity to work together, with the library clearly defining what behaviors are required, can help create trust between both parties.

As opposed to a suspension of privileges, cases of trespassing are ordinarily dealt with by law enforcement. Sometimes a suspension may lead to a trespass if a patron is unable to comply with the terms of their suspension (i.e., not being on library property until a reinstatement meeting has occurred). As we discussed above, it is important to utilize emergency services in these cases in a consistent way, so as to address bias that may occur.

INCIDENT DEBRIEFING

What Is Debriefing?

Debriefing is a structured review of an experience or incident after its occurrence. We know that libraries are not immune from potentially traumatic incidents involving violence or crises; debriefing is a strategy library systems can bring in to help decrease traumatization staff might experience. It provides individual staffers or the team with the opportunity to decompress and receive immediate feedback. A debrief is a supportive space in which to learn and prepare for the future. Debriefing may be one element of a more comprehensive incident response and intervention process. Additional follow-up may be necessary, depending on the severity of the event. It is crucial that library staff consult with experts for developing processes around debriefing. Some aspects of the information shared here fit within a standard supervisory relationship that leaders can and should use to support their staff. Formal debriefing is a specialized skill that professionals undergo additional training to perform. Do not use the information provided here as a stand-in for consultation and referral with experts. Consult with Human Resources and seek out supervisory and management training to learn more about what is within scope for library structures to support and what requires bringing in qualified professionals from outside of the library.

Why Is Debriefing Important?

Debriefing has shown to be a valuable tool in the workplace. It takes a bit of skill and intentional time, but is well worth the investment. Here are the benefits of debriefing:
- Removes uncertainty for staffers about their job responsibilities
- Enhances information retention
- Builds trust among staff
- Builds trust between staff and managers
- Promotes teamwork
- Helps provide closure
- Helps prevent burnout

Who, Where, and When?

Though a debrief can be a valuable element in the incident response process, it also has the potential to cause further disruption or harm if it is not used appropriately. For example, a debriefing conversation will not be helpful during an active crisis or with someone in an escalated state. For another example, a supervisor asking staff members debriefing questions on the library floor where patrons can overhear them does not create a sense of safety or trust. There are several important considerations for implementing a debrief, which are discussed below. When in doubt, consult with your library leadership or with Human Resources before proceeding with a debrief.

Who is the most appropriate person to lead the debrief?

Trained crisis responders recommend that a debrief should not be led by someone who was intimately involved in the incident. This is because it may be challenging to remain objective, and that person probably needs to participate in the debrief for their own benefit. Look for a leader or facilitator who has mediation skills, is familiar with the debrief purpose and model, and was not directly involved in the event. This could be a supervisor who was on-site but not part of the incident, or a social services professional on staff. Based on the severity of the incident and its scope of impact, it may be necessary to call in a facilitator from Human Resources or from outside the library system, such as a local mental health professional or an employee assistance program resource.

Where should the debrief take place?

A debrief should be a confidential process. It is crucial that the participants feel safe while talking honestly about their experience. They need to trust that what they say will not be shared without permission or used in a punitive way. Whether an individual or group debrief, conversations should be held in a space where the participants will not be overheard or observed by others who were not directly involved. Debriefs should take place in a professional space so as not to blur the lines between professional and personal support.

When should the debrief take place?

Ideally, debriefs should be held as soon as possible following a disruptive incident. This is because the incident's details and impact are still fresh in people's minds. That being said, the following elements need to be in place and may take time to coordinate:
- The immediate crisis has been resolved.
- Those impacted have returned to their emotional and cognitive baseline (and are no longer escalated or flooded).
- An appropriate facilitator has been identified.
- All impacted staff members are available to participate (this is especially important for group debriefs).

Who should be included in the debrief?

Any staff members who were directly involved in the event should be invited to participate in the debrief. Because there was a shared experience of trauma, it is important that there is the opportunity for a shared experience of resolution and healing. Attending a debrief should not be required, though, as people's process and comfort levels differ. Similarly, there should not be any requirement that attendees contribute verbally to the session. For some, simply being part of the process and hearing from colleagues can be valuable. It is not recommended that patrons participate in staff debriefs, even if the incident involved the public. Facilitating a mediation between patrons and other patrons or with staff is a different process. In that case, the staff may need a separate debrief in a follow-up to the mediation.

How is debriefing done?

A debriefing begins with a recap of the situation, the background, and key events that occurred. Everyone who was involved in the event is invited to share their experience of the event. You may explore what led up to the event, why it might have occurred, what role everyone played, what went well, and what did not go well. This review will likely result in a discussion of lessons learned and what should be done differently in the future. The debriefing should provide the opportunity for all participants to be heard. Effective debriefs allow participants to see the process as a learning opportunity, and not a punitive one.

Possible Debriefing Questions

Note: Facilitators don't have to ask all of these questions. Nor are these questions in a specific order. They are simply ideas to spark valuable conversation. Please remember that these are examples of questions that a trained professional might ask. Library staff may use them as ideas for how to discuss events with their colleagues; however, it is crucial to work within scope and receive training, consultation, and support around how to have these conversations. Often, supervisors and leaders will be best equipped to begin these conversations.

- What were your first thoughts about the incident once you got off the "autopilot" mode?
- What was the worst part of the event for you personally?
- What signs and symptoms of distress are you experiencing? (It is helpful to identify where in your body you feel things.)
- What's the one thing you personally are proudest of during this event?
- What's the one thing that surprised you most during this event?
- What did colleagues and/or supervisors do that was supportive?
- If you had a time machine, what's the one thing we can control as a team that you'd go back and do differently?
- What can we learn from this event?
- What should we do differently next time?
- What additional supports may be helpful to you and your fellow staff?

Follow-Up

A debriefing might lead to important follow-up actions. This could include tasks like incident reporting, referring to an employee assistance program, consulting with another department, or developing a self-care plan. What are the necessary next steps, and who will be responsible for them? You should set up accountability—identify actions, delegate tasks, set clear deadlines, and then agree on a time to check in about the status of the tasks.

BOUNDARIES

Maintaining healthy and appropriate boundaries is a basic tenet of social service provision in the library. This is especially important during assessment of a patron's needs. We want to make sure we are empowering patrons to do things for themselves (according to their ability) rather than accomplishing tasks for them. Doing "for" rather than "with" may be a disservice, as it does not invite the patron to learn and practice necessary life skills. We also need to protect ourselves from burnout, which can result from taking on more than we are capable of and have the capacity for. Boundaries are not just about one's ability to say "no." Boundaries include acknowledging and communicating one's own limitations. Consider the following guidelines:

- *Don't work harder than the patron.* Do "with" rather than "for." Advocacy can be helpful, but try not to become an intermediary between the patron and the social service resource. A good practice is that a librarian should not walk away from a patron conversation with a long to-do list.
- *Know your limitations.* If you are unsure about how to help with a particular issue, feel free to ask for help from others—coworkers, managers, a library social worker (if available), or community social service providers. Librarian social service referrals should be quick and easy. The tasks should wrap up with the conversation. When a situation becomes more complex, ask for assistance, or connect someone with an agency that might be able to address multiple needs.
- *People are resilient.* Worrying excessively about patrons can contribute to burnout. Of course, we are invested in the well-being of those we work with, but we must not fall into the trap of feeling that their well-being depends on our efforts. Remember that people have made it to this point using their existing resources and connections. Acknowledge and celebrate their successes—large and small.
- *It's okay to say "no."* It is always okay to say "no" to a request that makes you uncomfortable or that you may not be the best person to address. In these scenarios, consider asking a colleague to step in, consulting with a supervisor, or involving a social worker. If a patron is being disrespectful or offensive toward you, it is appropriate for you to set a boundary to protect and respect yourself.

CONFIDENTIALITY

Library and social work professionals highly value patrons' right to privacy and confidentiality. This can sometimes come into conflict with the need to know a patron's personal information in order to make a referral. For example, you might need to know a person's age in order to link them with an agency that has age requirements. Consider the following recommendations when personal information is required from a patron in order to connect them with a social service resource:

- Don't seek any more detailed information from a patron about a situation than is necessary for a referral. If the referral only requires knowing someone's age, ask specifically about age and explain why.
- Ask the patron to write down personal information so that other library users can't overhear. When finished, return the paper with the personal information back to the patron. If the patron instructs you to throw the paper away, tell them you will shred it and do so immediately.
- If a patron needs help making a phone call, encourage them to do as much of the talking as possible so they can decide what and how much information to share. Make every effort to provide access to a phone in a private location.
- Use discretion when talking with colleagues about patrons. It is natural to want to share patrons' needs, circumstances, and progress with coworkers. Remember that a patron chose to share their information with you specifically and did not assume you would tell other staff. Similarly, you don't want library users to overhear staff talking about patrons, as this might hurt their trust in the library. A patron's physical and emotional safety may be at risk if information spreads. If a coworker asks "What's going on with that patron?" or "How did that referral turn out?" you can respond with "I'd feel more comfortable keeping that person's information private," or "They were able to find what they needed." We acknowledge that sharing successes and debriefing difficult situations are important in the workplace. Try to think strategically about whom you seek support from, making sure to prioritize patron safety.

- How might you respond if a patron launches into sharing a lot of personal information or a story you haven't asked for? We've all been there. It is appropriate for you to set a boundary. You don't have to listen to information that is not relevant or comfortable for you. The following phrases may be helpful in this kind of situation.
    - "This is more information than I need to help you. I really need to know ____ so let's focus on that."
    - "I appreciate that you trust me. This is a lot of personal information that I don't feel comfortable talking about."
    - "I want to be respectful of your personal information and privacy. Let's talk about your library needs."
    - "I enjoy talking to you, but I need to transition to ____ (another task, a break, helping another patron)."

It is crucial to set these boundaries skillfully, as we do not want to shame someone for sharing their story with us; rather, we are hoping to model care while encouraging the patron to seek out the appropriate professionals to support their needs.

SELF-CARE

The way we care for ourselves directly impacts the way we care for others. It can be difficult to offer others patience and generosity if we ourselves feel depleted or neglected. You are undoubtedly familiar with the concept of self-care. It is likely that a well-meaning colleague, supervisor, or friend has encouraged you to set aside time for self-care as a way to remedy a difficult situation. You may be tired of hearing about self-care, or perhaps it feels like just one more thing to do; one more thing that *you* are responsible for. It can feel futile to try to care for ourselves when our stress is due in part to systems that are outside of our control.

We would like to challenge the notion that self-care requires a lot of effort. Self-care is something you have been doing your whole life—maybe without even recognizing it as such. Simply put, self-care is making an investment in your overall mental and physical well-being. It means doing what you can to ensure that your needs are taken care of. We often think of self-care as grandiose and indulgent—getting a massage or taking a vacation. These things are certainly restorative, but they're not always accessible. More often than not, self-care involves getting adequate sleep, eating foods that make us feel good, and taking medications as prescribed.

Additionally, self-care is not self-reliance. It does not happen in a vacuum, and we cannot be solely responsible for meeting all of our needs independently. Library systems need to actively encourage and support the wellness of their employees by building it into their culture and workday. Social connection is a critical part of mental and physical wellness. It is important to remain open to giving and receiving care and support from others. Let's give ourselves permission to lean on family, friends, colleagues, mentors, counselors, and medical professionals to bolster us.

Self-care is a "spectrum of decisions and actions that soothe and fortify us" against the challenges we encounter in the world.[1] There are small, simple practices we can utilize at home and at work to proactively energize and strengthen us. Self-care is not one-size-fits-all. It is important to figure out what helps your unique mind and body feel their best. We acknowledge that self-care practices are impacted by our access to resources and time.

Consider These Suggestions:

At home:
- Try to stick with a sleep routine.
- Pack lunch and snacks the night before work.
- Take medications as prescribed and stay connected with medical providers (as needed).
- Engage in physical activity.
- Maintain good hygiene.

ACTIVITY 3.3 • RESOURCE REFERRAL PRACTICE

You are working at the reference desk. A patron you've never met approaches and asks, "Hey, can you help me?" When you respond that you would be happy to assist, the patron says, "Can you tell me if there's a doctor nearby? I've gotta get some stuff checked out." What additional information do you need to make an effective referral?

- Has the patron seen a local doctor in the past? If so, they may be able to return to that provider.
- Is the patron looking for a primary care doctor or a specialist?
- Does the patron have medical insurance? You will want to find a clinic that accepts their insurance or takes uninsured patients, if necessary.
- Are there cultural considerations (translation services, culturally appropriate services, clinics that serve a specific racial or ethnic demographic)?
- Add further considerations here: _____

What potential barriers to accessing the resource should you ask about?

- Does the patron have a way to contact the clinic? Maybe they need to use a library phone.
- Does the patron have transportation to the clinic?
- Other barriers: _____

ACTIVITY 3.4 • SETTING BOUNDARIES PRACTICE

A regular patron, Max, has been looking for a job for several weeks. Max regularly updates you on his search—jobs he has applied for, asks you to review his resume, and so on. One afternoon, he excitedly shares that he has an interview the next day. Max also tells you that he does not have transportation to the interview. In the course of the conversation, you find out that the interview is before your shift starts at the library. Max asks whether you, or anyone you know, can meet him at the library and drive him to his appointment. If that won't work, he offers, maybe you can loan him money for a bus ticket.

What are some of the potential boundary concerns with this scenario?

_____
_____
_____

What questions can you ask Max to better understand the transportation challenge?

_____
_____
_____

What potential solutions can you offer to help Max get to his interview on time?

_____
_____
_____

- Engage in a centering practice, such as prayer, meditation, yoga, or listening to music.
- Make time for hobbies.
- Spend time with people you love and trust.
- Spend time with pets.
- Spend time in nature.

At work:
- Eat well and stay hydrated.
- Take breaks.
- Create a comfortable workspace. This may include an ergonomic setup, a file-organizing system, or displaying meaningful photos or quotes.
- Incorporate movement throughout the day. Alternate between sitting and standing, and walk around the building or take a stroll outside. Practice office stretches.
- Communicate with managers and colleagues.
- Participate in regular supervision to receive consultation and coaching to help you process your work experiences.
- Practice a transition ritual before or after shifts or when changing tasks. This could include a breathing exercise, meditation, self-affirmation, or changing out of work clothes when arriving home.

Rational detachment is a tool that is helpful for staying calm in difficult situations. Rational detachment is the ability to manage your own behavior and attitude and not take the behavior of others personally.[2] It involves shifting your focus from what is wrong with a situation to what you can do about it. Rational detachment is like a habit—the more you practice it, the more natural it will feel. It is important to identify strategies to practice at home and at work, like those listed above, that help maintain rational detachment. Applying these strategies can result in you feeling better equipped to manage disruptive situations at work and decrease the potential for burnout.

The Self-Care Plan

Maintaining and promoting our own wellness are crucial to helping foster resilience as library workers. One way to do this is to create and follow a self-care plan. A "self-care plan" is an organized plan or routine that you can implement to cultivate good habits for your overall health and well-being. It can help you manage stress and maintain professionalism. The plan invites you to identify activities and practices that have a positive impact in the short and long term. The plan may include your favorite nourishing activities, important reminders, and supportive people.

To develop your self-care plan, you should identify what you value and need in your daily life (maintenance self-care) and the strategies you can employ when or if you face a crisis along the way (emergency self-care). Everyone's self-care plan will be unique, but all plans involve making a commitment to attend to all the domains of your life—home, workplace, physical, psychological and emotional health, spiritual needs, and relationships.

A "self-care assessment" can help you highlight the good things you are already doing for yourself, and identify imbalances in the areas in which you practice self-care. The items in an assessment also provide ideas for new tools you may want to try to help prevent stress and burnout and to maintain and enhance your well-being. Use the checklist in "Exercise 3: Self-Care Assessment," to check in on your well-being practice.

NOTES

1. A. Borges, *The More or Less Definitive Guide to Self-Care*, illustrated ed. (New York: The Experiment, 2019), vii.
2. Crisis Prevention Institute, "The Road to Rational Detachment," *Crisis Prevention Institute* (blog), December 2, 2016, www.crisisprevention.com/Blog/Rational-Detachment.

PART II

STRATEGIES AND SCENARIOS

YOU HAVE NOW been exposed to a lot of information on providing what is essentially library customer service in a trauma-informed way. Using the information you have learned, you can help yourself, your patrons, and your community interact with the library in a way that minimizes the impacts of trauma and that may be safer for patrons who have experienced trauma. Using what you have learned, we invite you to practice your new skills by working through the scenarios in this part of the book. No one expects you to have this material completely absorbed or memorized, so please refer back to the early sections of the workbook and talk through this content with your colleagues.

Each of the scenarios in this part of the book uses a set of tools (or approaches) based on the Trauma Informed Care Project: *Reflect, Protect, Connect, Respect, and Redirect*.[1] These tools do not need to be completed in order to move on to the next; in some cases, you will use all of the tools, in other cases perhaps just one or two of them. The good news is there are many right ways to use these approaches.

Reflect asks you to consider the historical and cultural issues that may be involved in a situation at the library. *Protect* implores you to promote the physical and psychological safety of the people in your spaces. *Connect* suggests that you focus on the human-to-human relationships that staff have with a patron or group of patrons. *Respect* encourages you to engage in choice and collaboration with your patrons, so that they can be involved in deciding what their experience is at the library. And finally, *Redirect* encourages skill-building and confidence as patrons work through making their own decisions.

In this book, we have also examined other tools and techniques that employ the *Reflect, Protect, Connect, Respect, and Redirect* framework, as with reference interviews, suspensions, and bans, and whether and how to involve police and emergency responders. In the scenarios below, you are called to synthesize all of the information you have encountered. This is where the real learning happens, so dig in and work through each scenario. It's okay to feel unsure and uncomfortable; this work is not easy. Practicing here will set you up well to begin the work of incorporating trauma-informed principles in your work, and this, in turn, will be a small step to promoting wellness and resilience in your library community.

PART II • STRATEGIES AND SCENARIOS

TEN STEPS TO BUILDING SKILLS

The best way to develop skill in any area is to do the thing over and over again until it is practically second nature. As you experience various situations, and work through them, you become better and better at managing them.

NOTE

1. Trauma Informed Care Project, "Essential Components of Trauma Informed Judicial Practice," Orchard Place/Child Guidance Center, www.traumainformedcareproject.org/resources/Court%20Room%20TIC%20Sheet%20%20(002).pdf.

SCENARIO 1

Mental Health Challenges

DESCRIPTION: BECKY IS a regular patron who comes in every day and approaches the information desk to talk about her illness. According to Becky, Wi-Fi, cellphones, and electric-generated power sources make her sick. She is covered from head to toe to prevent these sources from entering her body. Becky talks about giving up her apartment to move back to the streets. She wants to find a place in the United States where Wi-Fi is not allowed. Becky always says that she cannot stay long, but you notice that she then goes to a computer and uses her cell phone to check on something.

CONNECT

How would you greet Becky and make her feel welcome?

Helpful Tips

- Address the patron by their first name if you know it.
- Maintain good eye contact if appropriate.
- Be warm and welcoming.

RESPECT

Do you use person-first language? Do you allow Becky to express her thoughts in a reasonable amount of time? Are you actively listening to what she is saying? What do you think about her use of the public computer and her cell phone? Is it appropriate to "diagnose" her?

Helpful Tips

- Be respectful and as reassuring as you can.
- Do not make assumptions about someone's life situation based on appearance, even though you might be correct. Do not assume the patron has mental health challenges, uses substances, is unhoused, or is a particular gender or sexual orientation. Remember that there are other possible explanations for someone's situation, such as their medical condition, developmental disabilities, trauma, or other challenges.
- Be patient. Do not rush the person because this may create anxiety.
- Be aware of your body language and tone of voice, as they may communicate more than what you say.

REFLECT

How does Becky's relationship with staff impact your interactions with her? Is there a shared history that can help her feel heard? What is the story you tell yourself about Becky? Is she a person who has a full life as well as an illness, or is she simply unwell?

Helpful Tips

- Forming relationships with all patrons can be important. You don't need to engage with Becky's hallucinations, but you can support her to find solutions about her concerns.
- Helping Becky work towards her goals may motivate her. She is in charge of her life and can decide what she wants to work on.
- It can be hard to spend a lot of time with a patron who presents with the same issues day after day. Consider how you can provide Becky with caring customer service while remaining available to other patrons.

PROTECT

What words can you use to convey to Becky that she is safe in the library? Are there current situations at the library that can put her sense of safety at risk? Can others overhear your conversation with Becky? How will you address inappropriate comments if a colleague or patron makes light of Becky's mental health challenges?

Helpful Tips

- Respect a patron's confidentiality at all times.
- Gently educate colleagues or other patrons who might say inappropriate things about Becky on how to respectfully work with patrons who are experiencing mental health challenges. Even unintentionally hurtful and derogatory words can be damaging.

REDIRECT

How would you respond to what Becky has shared about power sources, such as Wi-Fi, making her ill? What if she maintains that these are making her ill, and so the library needs to turn them off? How would you gently end the conversation? What steps will you take if Becky becomes angry or frustrated? Identify the challenges for you, as a library staff member, attending to a patron like Becky who presents with mental health issues. What do you think would be a good, reasonable outcome from such interactions?

Helpful Tips

- A hallucination is the experience of sensing or perceiving something that is not present in reality.[1] The perceptions can be visual, such as seeing things that are not there, or they can be auditory, such as hearing voices. Delusions, by contrast, are beliefs or belief systems that do not align with reality. Though mistaken, these perceptions and beliefs seem quite real to those experiencing them. It is not our role to try to convince the person that they are not real.
- In case of mental health challenges such as delusions or hallucinations, do not deny or contradict the patron's experiences. Gently redirect the patron to a topic or reference question you can assist them with. Convey your empathy through body language and tone of voice.
- Ask one question at a time and give the patron time to respond. If they do not appear to understand, repeat or use alternate words that might be easier to comprehend.
- Avoid offering more than one piece of information at a time. Providing too much information can be overwhelming and frustrating for the patron. Check to see that they understand the information offered.
- Break information into small, manageable steps. Be prepared to repeat steps if necessary. Remember that the patron might not be able to recall what you have just said.
- Respectfully disengage if the conversation does not serve the patron anymore or has become too lengthy.
- If the patron talks "off topic," patiently redirect them to the original, concrete topic.
- If the patron becomes angry, do not respond with anger. Continue to be in control and calm. Express empathy and acknowledge their anger and frustration.
- If the patron's angry or aggressive behavior becomes challenging or problematic, remember that you have the right to be safe, and to set limits on unacceptable behavior. Remain firm and polite. Express in clear and simple words what the patron is expected to do. It is best if you can provide a reason why you need the behavior to stop. For example, "Can you please lower your voice? I really would like to help you, but you might be asked to leave if you don't stop yelling," or "Please stop using inappropriate words. They are hurtful."

Additional Tips for Library Staff

- Be gentle with yourself by remembering that we all have limitations. Try to understand your own reactions and feelings.

Some of the most important services we provide include our compassion and recognition of our shared humanity.
- Plan for self-care during and after a difficult encounter.

NOTE

1. Andrew Rosenzweig, "Possible Causes of Hallucinations in Alzheimer's," Verywell Health, July 16, 2020, www.verywellhealth.com/causes-of-alzheimers-hallucinations-98577.

IN PRACTICE

Share the details of a time when a similar incident occurred at your library.

_____
_____
_____
_____
_____
_____
_____
_____

How was it resolved?

_____
_____
_____
_____
_____
_____
_____
_____

Using a trauma-informed lens and the ideals of Reflect, Protect, Connect, Respect, and Redirect, consider how the incident might have concluded differently.

_____
_____
_____
_____
_____
_____
_____
_____

SCENARIO 2

Sleeping at the Library

YOUR REGULAR PATRON, Angelica, appears to be sleeping in the quiet reading room. It is clear to you that she is breathing and is not disturbing anyone. Angelica has disclosed to you previously that she is unhoused.

REFLECT

What is your library's policy about sleeping? Is it implemented in the same way for all of your patrons? What is the impact of Angelica's behavior in the moment? What circumstances might cause her to have dozed off in the library?

Helpful Tips

- Many libraries have policies about sleeping in the library. The reality is that these policies are often implemented in a way that specifically targets patrons experiencing homelessness; library staff rarely wake up sleeping children or older adults with the same frequency as unhoused library users.
- The impact of a patron's behaviors can help you determine if intervention is needed. In this case, there is no disturbance. If Angelica were sleeping at a computer, she might be inadvertently preventing other patrons from accessing an important library resource.
- People experiencing homelessness are often prevented from getting restful sleep, if any sleep at all. Many are unable to sleep for more than two uninterrupted hours. Over time, this sleep deprivation can cause major health consequences, and some people simply cannot stay awake.
- In some cases, medications and other treatments can cause someone to be drowsy. You should review your ADA-accommodation procedures and work with your library's ADA coordinator or local ADA office to determine if an accommodation might be needed.

PROTECT

How can we help make sure Angelica is safe? Is she in medical distress? What signs can we look for to ensure she is okay?

Helpful Tips

- There are arguments on both sides of the sleeping issue. Keeping people awake is a sure way to know that they do not need medical help. Letting someone sleep, alternatively, can be considered humane, given the damaging realities of sleep deprivation.
- Breath and occasional movement may be indicators that a person is simply asleep. Unusual postures and a lack of movement for a prolonged period may be warning signs that medical care is needed.
- Consider consulting with local emergency medical services to receive guidance on what to look for when someone is sleeping and when to call for help.

CONNECT

In waking someone, how can you approach them so as not to startle them? If they do not respond to verbal cues, what other strategies can you use that don't involve touching them?

Helpful Tips

- Anyone, in addition to people who have experienced trauma, may have a strong startle response at being woken up. Keeping distance between yourself and the sleeping person when trying to wake them up can help prevent unintended injury.
- Do not touch a sleeping person. Unwanted touching can be a trigger and may create risk for your library. If needed, you might try tapping the chair or desk that they are using. Be aware that these strategies may be interpreted as aggressive, however.
- Be mindful of the words you use to wake someone. Jokes and other remarks may seem funny in the moment, but can be damaging to an ongoing working relationship with the patron and other patrons in similar identity groups.

RESPECT

What is the relationship you have with this patron? How can you foster trust?

Helpful Tips

- If you have a relationship with this patron, leverage it when speaking with them to let them know you are concerned for their welfare. In a kind way, state the reasons for waking them.
- If you do not have a relationship with the patron, consider how they might view the interaction based on assumptions you might be making about them. If they present with visible signifiers of homelessness, they may feel targeted and that the library does not respect their situation.

REDIRECT

Does Angelica need to leave for the day? Are there resources that might be needed? What strategies can you use to help her stay awake?

Helpful Tips

- If your library policy is such that Angelica is asked to leave, perhaps after several requests to stay awake, try to ensure that she is aware of the policy. People who don't get regular sleep sometimes are unable to remember having been informed of policies previously. If Angelica was told last week, she may be physiologically unable to recall that now. Also, survival is going to be a higher priority for her than keeping track of library policies.
- Consider that Angelica may need help connecting to resources for housing and shelter, if she has not already engaged these systems. She may share a very real belief that it is more difficult or less safe to sleep in a shelter than elsewhere. She has the right to decide what is right for her.
- You can brainstorm ideas with Angelica about how she can stay awake while in the library. Consider asking her what may have worked for her before, or make a few recommendations as to what you've seen work well (going outside for a moment, splashing water on your face, providing something to read). Remember to use respectful and non-patronizing language when making recommendations. Angelica is deserving of respect and consideration.

PART II • STRATEGIES AND SCENARIOS

IN PRACTICE

Share the details of a time when a similar incident occurred at your library.

_____
_____
_____
_____
_____
_____
_____

How was it resolved?

_____
_____
_____
_____
_____
_____
_____

Using a trauma-informed lens and the ideals of Reflect, Protect, Connect, Respect, and Redirect, consider how the incident might have concluded differently.

_____
_____
_____
_____
_____
_____
_____
_____
_____

SCENARIO 3

Strong Personal Odor

A PATRON APPROACHES you with a disgusted look on their face. They say, "Over at the computers there's a guy who smells so bad. I can't stand to be over there. Can you tell him to leave so I can get back to my work?"

There are two patrons to address in this scenario: the patron who made the complaint and the patron with reported poor hygiene. Consider how you can respond thoughtfully and effectively to both of them.

REFLECT

Reflect on your thoughts and feelings about these patrons. Do you take the report at face value? Do you have assumptions or hesitations about approaching the patron with reportedly poor hygiene? How might these feelings impact the way you respond?

Helpful Tips

- Try to imagine the experience of the patron with poor hygiene. Why might they be in this situation? How might they feel about their condition: embarrassed, helpless, unaware? How do you think they are often treated? This imagining—instead of assuming—will help you develop empathy.
- Ask yourself questions to identify your personal biases before responding to the complaint:
    - Have I encountered a situation like this before? How did it go?
    - Am I more sympathetic toward one of these patrons than the other?
    - Do I feel comfortable initiating a conversation about hygiene? Why or why not?
    - Do I have assumptions about someone with poor hygiene? These could be negative, such as "they're probably making bad life choices," or well-intentioned, such as "their life must be so hard. I feel bad for them."

PROTECT

It is important to consider the physical and emotional privacy, dignity, and comfort of both patrons in this situation. Physical considerations include assessing whether the patrons' basic needs are being met. Library furniture and surfaces may need cleaning. Emotional considerations include speaking quietly about the situation to maintain privacy, not sharing information between patrons, and showing respect rather than disgust.

Helpful Tips

- Respond to the complaint in a neutral way. It is not necessary (or respectful) to align with the complainant's perspective with a response like, "Oh that sounds icky. I don't blame you for moving." Instead, you might say, "Thank you for letting me know. I'll look into that."
- The patron making the complaint does not need to know how the situation is resolved. If they ask follow-up questions, provide a generic response like "your concern has been addressed."
- It is possible the patron making the complaint will have opinions or questions about who is welcome in the library. They may say, "This library used to be nicer before people from the shelter came in," or "Why do you guys put up with people making a mess here?" It is important to be familiar with and clearly explain library policies to the patron.

PART II • STRATEGIES AND SCENARIOS

CONNECT

Remember that it is your job to address behavior separately from individuals. People are welcome in the library. Disruption is not. How can you approach the patron in question with respect and care? Use words and a tone that convey a desire to understand and assist, rather than judge.

Helpful Tips

- When approaching a patron with reported poor hygiene, do a scan of the area. If other library users might overhear your conversation, ask the patron to step aside with you.
- Point out the concerning behavior you notice. You might address the "strong odor coming from your clothing" instead of the "bad smell coming from you."
- Speak only for yourself. You could say, "I notice a strong odor coming from your clothes" rather than "other patrons are complaining about how you smell." You want to avoid creating tension between patrons or make someone feel ashamed of their impact on others.

RESPECT

As much as possible, engage patrons in collaborative problem-solving. Try to be creative. The goal is to keep people in the library and help them be successful in using the library's services.

Helpful Tips

- Be aware of your tone and body language. Are you communicating respect or judgment? Pay attention to facial expressions and your physical distance in an attempt to avoid the odor.
- If policy requires a patron to leave the library, focus on behavior. For example, "We'll be happy to have you back in the library after your things are cleaned up," versus "You can come back when you smell better."
- Be thoughtful about if and how you talk about this situation with colleagues. A comment like "I had to talk with a guy who smelled so bad!" can negatively impact the work environment. Though a patron may not overhear what is said, disrespectful and judgmental conversations among the staff can affect library culture.

REDIRECT

Your goal is to help patrons find information about a variety of subjects. When challenges arise, offer patrons options and autonomy. Respect their choices even if you do not understand or agree with them.

Helpful Tips

- How can odor be addressed without asking the patron to leave the library? Can they check out a laptop in a private study room so others are not disrupted? Can you offer sanitizing wipes for them to clean their belongings?
- Ask if the patron would like a list of local resources based upon their stated needs: laundry or shower facilities, clothing banks, and so on. If requested, print out and provide recommendations. Approaching a patron with unwanted resources from the start could be interpreted as condescending.
- Ask if there are barriers to accessing resources. Perhaps the patron needs a bus map or ticket. Address these barriers as you are able.
- It is the patron making the complaint who wants something to change. What options can you offer that patron? A laptop in a study room or a different computer station? Be careful about drawing attention to "problem" patrons unnecessarily if they are having a successful, satisfying experience.

IN PRACTICE

Share the details of a time when a similar incident occurred at your library.

_____
_____
_____
_____
_____
_____
_____

How was it resolved?

_____
_____
_____
_____
_____
_____
_____

Using a trauma-informed lens and the ideals of Reflect, Protect, Connect, Respect, and Redirect, consider how the incident might have concluded differently.

_____
_____
_____
_____
_____
_____
_____
_____

SCENARIO 4

Personal Belongings

A YOUNG, BLACK, gender diverse-presenting patron you've never seen before enters your library. They are carrying two large camping backpacks and several smaller bags. They place their items near a study table and go to use a computer a few yards away. Their belongings are obstructing the walkway and preventing others from using the study table. This behavior is not in compliance with your library's patron code of conduct.

REFLECT

How does this person's identity impact your reaction to this situation? Systemic inequities cause young people of color to be at risk for homelessness at much higher rates than their white counterparts. Additionally, members of the LGBTQ community are at greater risk for homelessness due to social inequities. Though we can't ascertain someone's housing status by looking at them, it is possible that housing insecurity is at play here. Would your reaction change if this patron were older, or elderly? Male, or female? What if they were white, or Latinx? Our personal stories, biases, and work histories can impact how we respond to individuals experiencing hardship.

Helpful Tips

- Make sure to review the policies your library has that govern this sort of behavior. Are they equitable?
- Consider that there are groups that might be targeted more, like those who carry their belongings with them, as opposed to parents who carry an equal amount of childcare supplies.
- Think about how your library and your community treat people who have the identities this patron presents with. Consider the larger systems that may be at play in this patron's life.

PROTECT

How can you support this patron's need to keep their belongings safe while using the library? How might you be able to facilitate arranging the space so that walkways are not blocked?

Helpful Tips

- Consider the balance between supporting this person's needs while ensuring other library users' safety and access to resources. What other locations are available for storing this person's belongings?
- Understand that it's the belongings being in the way that needs to change. The patron is welcome in the library.

CONNECT

Because this person appears to be new to the library, welcome them in. Introduce yourself and provide information about the services available. You have the opportunity to set the tone for how this patron may view the library in the future.

Helpful Tips

- Creating a connection or relationship with someone is simply the humane choice. In an ideal world, we'd be able to welcome everyone in our spaces.

- Remember that a power differential exists between library staff and patrons. They may see you as an authority figure and therefore a threat.
- Having a friendly conversation opens the door for sharing behavior expectations. Patrons will probably not be aware of what the requirements are for personal belongings, even if they are posted on a sign or spelled out on a website.
- Sharing observations in a neutral way can help transition a conversation from introduction to problem-solving. This could look like, "I see you have a lot of bags with you today." This provides the patron an opportunity to reflect on their belongings or circumstances; if they don't, staff can then steer the conversation towards the library policy.
- Engaging with a patron in this way can open the door to some resource reference questions. The patron may share a need, or you may tentatively offer an idea that opens doors to connecting with needed community resources.

RESPECT

Approach this patron as an individual and valued community member. How can you demonstrate understanding that they are a human being, and not simply the source of all the bags? How can you have a conversation with them about the changes that are needed for safety and access in a way that doesn't call them out in front of other patrons or infantilize them? How can you respond to this patron equitably, so that they have service consistent with what you can provide to all your patrons?

Helpful Tips

- By sharing your name and pronouns first, you are opening a door to conversation. If the patron is not interested, or doesn't want to share their personal information, respect that choice.
- Consider who else is around when you are engaging in conversation. What space is available that might be more private, if needed?
- You don't need to know specific details of their circumstances if they don't want to share these with you. Allow them to make choices about what information they share.

REDIRECT

What possible solutions exist for the immediate issue of bags blocking walkways? Brainstorm solutions to the safety risk and allow for choice.

Helpful Tips

- Avoid command and demand language like, "You need to move these now."
- Allow the patron to choose what solution works best for them. It may be that they choose to leave for the day.
- Remember that the patron has many strengths and may have ideas about how to resolve their concerns that you have not thought of.

PART II • STRATEGIES AND SCENARIOS

IN PRACTICE

Share the details of a time when a similar incident occurred at your library.
_____
_____
_____
_____
_____
_____
_____

How was it resolved?
_____
_____
_____
_____
_____
_____
_____

Using a trauma-informed lens and the ideals of Reflect, Protect, Connect, Respect, and Redirect, consider how the incident might have concluded differently.
_____
_____
_____
_____
_____
_____
_____
_____

Suspected Intoxication, Under the Influence

YOU NOTICE A patron sitting at a computer with his eyes closed. He slowly slumps forward until his forehead is touching the keyboard, and then he jerks back up to a sitting position. He appears to be mumbling. His face is flushed. You approach the patron to offer assistance. You think he says his name is Mitchell, but his speech is difficult to understand. After you introduce yourself he asks, "Who are you? What is this place?" He is clearly disoriented.

REFLECT

Take a moment to consider if you may have any bias or preconceived ideas about Mitchell and his situation. What factors might affect how you respond to him and the kind of service you provide? Self-awareness is a tool that can prompt you to intentionally enter a situation with a mindset toward success. Let go of any assumptions you might have before interacting. Self-reflection might clarify that you are not the appropriate person to respond for a variety of reasons.

Helpful Tips

Ask yourself the following questions to identify any personal bias and assess your capacity to respond in a professional, appropriate way:
- Have I interacted with this patron before? How did it go? Do I have positive, negative, or neutral feelings toward them?
- If I've addressed situations like this in the past, how did they go? Did I feel successful, satisfied, frustrated, helpless, or confused? Am I assuming the same outcome here?
- What are my thoughts and feelings about Mitchell's gender, age, appearance, and behavior?
- Am I nervous or afraid to approach this patron? What am I afraid might happen?
- What kind of day am I having? Do I have the energy and patience necessary to respond with clear thinking and kindness? If not, who can assist?

PROTECT

Mitchell's behavior may be cause for concern. What are the potential causes of his lethargy and disorientation? He could be impacted by low blood sugar, dementia, exhaustion, medication side effects, or substance use. How can you assess and address his physical and emotional safety, including his privacy? Do you need to consider the safety of others?

Helpful Tips

- If you are concerned that a person is unwell, try to gather information about what might be affecting their behavior. After introducing yourself, you may ask how they are feeling and whether they need anything. You could ask whether they've had something to eat or drink recently or if they've been able to sleep lately.
- Protect the person's privacy and confidentiality. If you need to ask personal questions to assess safety, try to keep the conversation quiet. Do not share information about the person or situation with other patrons or staff unless doing so is necessary to resolve the situation.
- Ensure the safety of other people. Is a person's behavior affecting those around them? It may be necessary to move to a private place or ask others to leave the area.

- There may be times when you don't feel comfortable addressing patron behavior. There may also be times when you are not the most appropriate or effective person to respond. It is okay to set up boundaries for yourself and ask colleagues to step in.

CONNECT

How would you start a conversation with Mitchell? How can you communicate that you are available to provide help if needed? Do you feel comfortable approaching him on your own?

Helpful Tips

- Introduce yourself as a library staff member and provide your name.
- Move toward people in a safe, nonthreatening way. Be aware of their personal space and belongings. Approach from the front or side. Approaching from behind may be startling or even frightening. Do not touch their body or belongings.
- Use a warm, low tone of voice. People who appear confused, disoriented, or lethargic respond best to a quiet voice. Speak slowly and clearly, use very few words.
- If you are uncomfortable approaching someone on your own, consider asking a colleague to accompany you or observe your interaction from a distance.

RESPECT

How can you offer assistance without judging Mitchell's behavior or assuming its cause? Invite Mitchell to identify what he needs. What options can you provide? How can you encourage Mitchell to determine what is best for himself?

Helpful Tips

- Address the behavior rather than assuming its cause. You might say "I notice you seem to be having a hard time staying awake," rather than "Have you been using drugs?"
- Let people know specifically how you can assist them. Offer options. You might say "Can I help you find a more comfortable chair?"

REDIRECT

What resources can you offer Mitchell while he is in the library? Do you need to make referrals to community providers? What policies, procedures, and laws apply to this situation?

Helpful Tips

- Know your internal resources, including what is available to meet people's basic needs in the library. Someone with limited access to food resources may feel much better if you can provide them with a snack.
- Know external and community resources. Where is the nearest food bank and what are its hours? What local substance-use treatment clinics accept state insurance? If someone needs a referral or connection to a community provider, it is most effective to provide them with information immediately. You might offer to help a person make a call to the resource.
- Be familiar with and adhere to library policies and procedures. You want to feel confident when responding to difficult situations such as medical emergencies or open alcohol containers.
- Remember to address only behavior that is disruptive, unsafe, or unlawful. This may be different than behavior that conflicts with your personal values and beliefs. If you suspect that someone may be under the influence of substances but their behavior is not disruptive, unsafe, or outside library policy, it is not appropriate to draw attention to them.
- As much as possible, provide options and let people determine what is best for them. Notify them of your actions. You might say, "I'm concerned about your health because

SCENARIO 5 • SUSPECTED INTOXICATION, UNDER THE INFLUENCE

you're having a hard time staying awake and you told me you're on new medication. I'd like to call a medical professional to come check on you. I will sit with you until they arrive. Is that okay?" Another example is, "Open containers of alcohol are not allowed in the library. You can choose to throw that can away or finish it outside."

IN PRACTICE

Share the details of a time when a similar incident occurred at your library.

_____
_____
_____
_____
_____
_____
_____

How was it resolved?

_____
_____
_____
_____
_____
_____
_____

Using a trauma-informed lens and the ideals of Reflect, Protect, Connect, Respect, and Redirect, consider how the incident might have concluded differently.

_____
_____
_____
_____
_____
_____
_____
_____

SCENARIO 6

Substance Use

A PATRON APPROACHES you at the service desk to report that there's someone "using drugs" in the bathroom. You thank the patron for the information and say library staff will look into it. Before going to the bathroom, you enlist another staff member to accompany you, and you bring your emergency kit and cell phone. You knock on the door, enter, and see there's one person seated on the floor of a stall.

REFLECT

There are a lot of factors to consider in this scenario. Substance use, whether alcohol, marijuana, or illicit substances, on the premises of the library is typically a library policy violation, in addition to being illegal behavior. Occasionally, someone using substances may need emergency medical help, depending on their level of intoxication. It may be that the person is interested in substance use treatment, or they may have no current interest in these services. Another consideration is the concept of harm reduction, which is a public health ideology that aims to minimize harm from substance use. Harm reduction philosophy acknowledges that people use substances and aims to keep the user as safe as possible. Harm reduction strategies might include using around others, acquiring clean syringes or needles, or carrying opioid overdose reversal medication, Naloxone or Narcan.

What policies and procedures does your library have with regard to substance use in the library? Are they punitive? Do they allow for harm reduction and recovery? Are different kinds of substance use in the library treated differently? What resources are nearby about which you can provide patrons with information?

Helpful Tips

- People who use drugs are complex and multifaceted, mirroring how substance use is a complex and multifaceted issue. Approach them from a place of care and respect.
- It is not your job to stop someone from using substances. People who stop their use or decrease their use of drugs or alcohol often do so by choice, with the assistance of trained professionals and others who are supportive.

PROTECT

What is the scene inside the bathroom? What substances are being used? Does the patron respond when you speak to them? Do they need medical help?

Helpful Tips

- This patron's physical safety is the highest priority. Bringing a cell phone to be able to call for emergency services quickly, in addition to an emergency kit that contains Narcan, are two strategies aimed at life-saving.
- As we know, a report of someone "using drugs" can vary from relatively innocuous to life-threatening, depending on the substance and circumstances. Being prepared can make a big difference when responding in the moment.
- Avoid the urge to jump to punishment or consequences right away. Someone using in the library may be doing so as a way to help minimize the harm of using alone. If the patron's safety is not at immediate risk, you can ask them to leave for the day (if that

is library policy). Consider providing them with information on who to connect with when they return to discuss safe library use. If there is an immediate risk to safety, do not kick them out of the library. Call emergency medical services as you would for any other medical crisis.
- Never restrain a person who insists on leaving. If they leave, call emergency services anyway and give them any information you have about where they appeared to be going.

CONNECT

How would you approach this person? Given that they may be intoxicated, how can you be respectful and give yourself a better chance of being understood? What is most important in the moment?

Helpful Tips

- Approach from the front, if possible, and announce yourself and colleague as library staff. You can say that you were told someone was using drugs in the bathroom, and that you are there to see if they might need help.
- Begin from a place of concern for their well-being.
- Ask straightforward, open questions to get the information you need. Allow for silence if needed.
- If there are other patrons in the bathroom, you might consider asking them to step out in order to keep the interaction safe and confidential.

RESPECT

How can you acknowledge this patron's humanity in the moment? How will you talk about this situation to emergency responders or colleagues? How can you preserve this individual's dignity?

Helpful Tips

- Be aware of being judgmental, condescending, or using shaming language.
- Share truthful, non-blaming observations of what you see. You don't need someone to confess to using if you have not seen them do so. However, you can share the reasons why you might be taking your next steps: "I see several empty beer cans," "I can see and smell smoke in here," or "You have a needle in your hand."
- Clearly communicate your expectations regarding behavior that is or is not appropriate in the library. You can let the person know that they are not allowed to use substances in the library. Remember, everyone is welcome in the library. Certain behaviors are not.

REDIRECT

What resources can you provide this patron while they are in the library? Where can someone go in your community who is looking for detox services? If they are open to other help, do you know who to refer them to? If they don't want substance use support today, how can you help them follow procedures for safe use of the library in the future?

- As always, offering choices is a helpful way for someone to regain a sense of autonomy. If the person is interested in referrals, see how they would like to receive the information.
- Having flyers or cards with substance treatment information on them can be useful for these moments.
- When implementing library policy, consider that someone may rely on library services like internet and phone use to be able to engage with recovery and treatment supports.

IN PRACTICE

Share the details of a time when a similar incident occurred at your library.
_____
_____
_____
_____
_____
_____
_____

How was it resolved?
_____
_____
_____
_____
_____
_____
_____

Using a trauma-informed lens and the ideals of Reflect, Protect, Connect, Respect, and Redirect, consider how the incident might have concluded differently.
_____
_____
_____
_____
_____
_____
_____
_____

Threatening Verbal and Nonverbal Behavior

YOU CAN HEAR a regular patron, Marcus, yelling at a patron using one of the computers. Marcus is arguing that this patron is using the computer he likes to use, and that he had better move quickly "or else!" He lunges toward the patron at the computer. The other patron says, "What's your problem, man? There's like three open ones right now!"

REFLECT

Is this behavior typical for Marcus? If so, what strategies have worked well to help de-escalate him in the past? If not, what strategies have worked well for de-escalating other patrons? Marcus's behavior might seem like an overreaction, given that there are other open computers. What could another patron using his favorite computer mean to him? How might Marcus's identity presentations, like race and gender, affect how you approach him?

Helpful Tips

- Be aware of your own biases about the kind of behavior you expect from certain patrons. Where did those stories come from, and are they true?
- Reflection before stepping in to help de-escalate this situation must occur quickly, or it just may not be possible in the moment. It can be important to revisit these questions after a solution has been reached and when everyone is feeling calmer. This is when some of our best learning can happen.

PROTECT

How can you work toward both the other patron's and Marcus's physical safety? Does the confrontation need to move away from the computers? How can you help create physical space between the patrons (and between them and you)? Are there other people or furniture nearby that may need to be moved out of the way?

Helpful Tips

- Physical safety is the highest priority. This situation is a high-stakes one, but it is not yet a crisis: the goal is to de-escalate and keep anyone from being injured.
- Enlist the help of other coworkers to assist you if needed.
- Avoid physical touching if possible. When someone is escalated, being touched can cause a physical altercation to occur where it may not have otherwise.

CONNECT

Marcus is having a big reaction to his favorite computer being used by someone else. What could we say that helps him understand the importance he is placing on this particular computer, while balancing other library users' needs?

Helpful Tips

- Acknowledge the frustration Marcus is feeling. Consider acknowledging the perceived reality that he uses this computer so much that it has started to feel like his own personal machine.
- Offer to work together with Marcus to find a solution.
- Validate Marcus's concerns, while making sure that safety is the focus. "I can see how upset this is making you. Let's give everyone some space so no one gets hurt while we figure this out."

RESPECT

How can you respect Marcus's desire for a specific computer while maintaining equal access to library resources for all patrons? There may be some very specific reasons why Marcus prefers this computer—how can we support those ideas in another area? Additionally, other patrons may suggest to you that Marcus is being "crazy" or "acting like a baby." When the situation has resolved, how will you talk or write about this incident? Though Marcus's concerns may seem blown out of proportion to library staff, it is important to use neutral and respectful language both during and after an incident.

Helpful Tips

- Consider how you let Marcus know what behavior expectations the library has for its patrons in a way that is not demeaning.
- Be aware of how you talk about this situation to other people, both patrons and staff.
- Avoid belittling the problem or judging Marcus's concern.
- Treat both patrons with respect and dignity as you work toward a solution.

REDIRECT

Address threatening behavior to help de-escalate the situation. It may take a little time and communication to help Marcus calm down and feel safe. How can you help Marcus find another computer?

Helpful Tips

- Creating space and removing triggers can be useful in starting a conversation. Consider moving away from the computers to have a discussion where the other patron and the computer at issue aren't so stimulating.
- See what library needs Marcus has. Try to find another way to help him use the library today that does not involve a specific machine.
- Let Marcus know that threatening others is not okay, and that it makes the library community feel unsafe. Encourage other ways he can share his concerns with library staff without yelling at or lunging at other patrons.

IN PRACTICE

Share the details of a time when a similar incident occurred at your library.

_____
_____
_____
_____
_____
_____
_____

How was it resolved?

_____
_____
_____
_____
_____
_____
_____

Using a trauma-informed lens and the ideals of Reflect, Protect, Connect, Respect, and Redirect, consider how the incident might have concluded differently.

_____
_____
_____
_____
_____
_____
_____
_____

SCENARIO 8

Unsheltered Teens

YOU NOTICE THAT Sharif, one of your teen volunteers, has been bringing a large backpack into the library every day after school. When he opens it, you see that it is full of clothes. You ask Sharif how he is doing, and he tells you that his parents have been fighting a lot and he felt he had no choice but to leave the house.

REFLECT

How is this new information about Sharif impacting you? Is his experience connecting to relationships or situations in your own life that you have strong feelings about? For example, maybe you have a nephew his age. Or perhaps a close childhood friend stayed with your family because their home was unsafe. Maybe you grew up with parents who fought often. Are you likely to respond to Sharif with emotion or practicality? You have a good relationship with him and are invested in his well-being, so how can you communicate care, provide assistance, and remain professional?

Helpful Tips

- Maintain the boundaries of your professional role. What kind of response is and is not appropriate? Helping Sharif call local youth shelters (if he wants to pursue that option) could be helpful. Offering to drive him to a shelter in your personal vehicle is outside your scope as a library staffer, however.
- Be aware of any biases you may have about a patron's ability to make good decisions for themselves based upon their age or other factors. Respect their autonomy and freedom of choice.
- If Sharif's experience has similarities to your own, remember that everyone feels and processes things differently. You don't want to assume that you understand what he is going through or that you know what is best for him.

PROTECT

How can you help ensure Sharif's safety outside of the library? How can you help facilitate his basic needs being met? What response fits within your role, and why is it important to maintain professional boundaries?

Helpful Tips

- Safety is a high priority. If you believe someone may be in danger, help them identify and access the necessary social service resources.
- Protect patrons, yourself, and your library system by staying within your scope and role. Avoid trying to provide consultation that is outside of your training. Examples of working outside of your scope could include advising someone on how to respond to an unsafe home situation or how to manage a mental illness.
- Refer and defer to appropriate professional supports.

CONNECT

Sharif shared sensitive personal information. How might you help him feel safe? How can you communicate that you can and want to help?

Helpful Tips

- Acknowledge people's courage in sharing personal information. Thank them for trusting you.
- Validating someone's experience shows that you are listening to and *hearing* them. You might say "I imagine that situation would be scary," or "I hear that you're feeling worn out from so much transition."
- Assure the person that you are available to help now and in the future.
- Consider your role and relationship. Are you the most appropriate support person to continue a conversation or respond to a need? It may be necessary to hand off to a colleague with whom the person has a trusting relationship or who has relevant expertise. Self-awareness is important here. If you think it may be challenging for you to maintain professional boundaries, you may want to refer out.

RESPECT

How can you respect Sharif's autonomy while offering help? What are your thoughts about privacy and confidentiality?

Helpful Tips

- Consider what and how much information you need to help with a difficult situation. Though library staff are trusted community helpers, they are not counselors, so less information may be more in order to protect a person's emotional well-being. For example, you don't necessarily need to know why someone feels unsafe at home in order to provide them with shelter referrals.
- Be aware of physical space and people within hearing distance of your conversation. You want to ensure privacy for sensitive issues.
- Avoid passing judgement or giving advice. Statements such as "I'm sure it's better to stay with your parents than be on the streets," or "You really should talk to your parents about how you feel" may push people away or cause mistrust.
- Ask open-ended questions to gather necessary information. Examples include "How can I best support you?" or "What is the most important need you have today? Maybe I can help."

REDIRECT

What shelter resources are available for Sharif? What partner agencies can you refer him to? Perhaps your city has a centralized process for connecting youths to safe shelter. Does your library maintain an electronic or print list of local social service organizations for staff and patrons to access?

Helpful Tips

- You should develop and maintain relationships with local social service agencies. Try to become familiar with their hours, programs, and referral processes so you can provide accurate information to patrons.
- Develop an efficient way for library staff to store and access information about social service resources. This could involve utilizing county-curated databases, maintaining an internal database, or having print materials readily available.
- Consider whether your library needs to develop protocols for supporting unsheltered youth. It is important to ensure that staff are trained on relevant workflows.

PART II • STRATEGIES AND SCENARIOS

IN PRACTICE

Share the details of a time when a similar incident occurred at your library.

_____
_____
_____
_____
_____
_____
_____
_____

How was it resolved?

_____
_____
_____
_____
_____
_____
_____
_____

Using a trauma-informed lens and the ideals of Reflect, Protect, Connect, Respect, and Redirect, consider how the incident might have concluded differently.

_____
_____
_____
_____
_____
_____
_____
_____

SCENARIO 9

Adult Self-Neglect

MISS TIFFANY IS a regular patron of your branch. She has been coming to the library every Tuesday and Thursday morning for years, and often remarks that she is an "institutional icon." Miss Tiffany is an older adult and has typically been active and boisterous. Over the last month, however, her presentation has changed drastically. She has become very thin and her personal hygiene is poor; she has worn the same outfit for weeks, and it is now very dirty. Her communication has changed, and she has difficulty answering questions. You have asked her if she needs help at home, and she brushes you off.

REFLECT

What impression is this change in Miss Tiffany's behavior making on you? How have you come to your own beliefs about aging? Might there be a cultural component to how Miss Tiffany is acting that you are not aware of? How has the library engaged with older adults in the past?

Helpful Tips

- It is important to gain an understanding of our own personal history and beliefs about aging. Think about your experiences with aging—either yours, or that of your friends and relatives. Try to cultivate an awareness of any biases you may have.
- Consider reaching out to local experts and service providers for education on the aging process. Each state has different requirements for reporting elder and at-risk adult abuse. There are supports available, and your library needs to be familiar with them.

- Find out how the library has (or has not) responded in situations similar to these. How might library confidentiality come into play in your library's response to Miss Tiffany?

PROTECT

Is Miss Tiffany in danger? Based on what you're observing, what health and wellness implications might there be? How can you help make sure that her basic needs (food, clothing, hygiene) are being met? What are the at-risk adult services and reporting requirements in your area?

Helpful Tips

- There is a real risk that Miss Tiffany is unwell and unable to care for herself. And she may not be able to ask for the help she might need.
- Consult with your library's leadership about your concerns regarding Miss Tiffany's well-being. They can help you understand the library's role in supporting at-risk older patrons.
- Consult with local providers to get a sense for appropriate next steps. Refer and defer to the appropriate responders and supports.

CONNECT

Miss Tiffany is a longtime patron, and you and many of your staff have a relationship with her. You may decide to speak with her about your concerns. Kindly share your observations that she has been behaving differently recently. Let her know that the library cares and would like to help.

Helpful Tips

- It can be scary to start a conversation like this one. As a member of the library community, Miss Tiffany has come to rely on and expect a certain type of normal, everyday engagement with library staff. This conversation may be a departure from that.
- Your extra engagement is grounded in concern for her well-being. You don't have to convince her that she is either well or unwell. Your role is to try to connect her to the support services that could assist her.

RESPECT

How can you respect Miss Tiffany's rights to privacy and autonomy? You may determine that a report or referral is required, based on your area's laws and best practices for protecting older adults. How can you make that referral in a way that is respectful?

Helpful Tips

- Though you may be acting on behalf of Miss Tiffany and sharing some information with others that she would prefer not to be shared, you should keep as much of her information protected as you can. There is a balance between sharing enough information to keep her safe and sharing everything you might be aware of.
- If possible, you should work in partnership with Miss Tiffany in filing a report or a referral. You can let her know that based on the behaviors you've observed, the library is hoping to connect her with helpers. You can give her a summary of what information you will share and explain that you are doing so to help keep her safe.
- Be kind, firm, and clear. Avoid making bargains or promises about what you need to see, or will or will not do. Remember, in consultation with experts, that you are following best practices for helping older adults in your community.

REDIRECT

Providing opportunities for choice and respecting decision-making can be key in helping Miss Tiffany navigate support and care. Though some aspects of the situation are nonnegotiable (like connecting with helpers), there may be opportunities for Miss Tiffany to help decide how this is done. She may prefer working with a particular agency, family member, or type of helper.

Helpful Tips

- Be clear on what you insist on. Where matters of life and health are not at risk, allow for patrons to make appropriate choices, if they can.
- Focus on strengths. Every person in our community has abilities and skills that have helped them, and Miss Tiffany is no exception. How can we leverage her experience and expertise to help herself?

SCENARIO 9 • ADULT SELF-NEGLECT

IN PRACTICE

Share the details of a time when a similar incident occurred at your library.

___

How was it resolved?

___

Using a trauma-informed lens and the ideals of Reflect, Protect, Connect, Respect, and Redirect, consider how the incident might have concluded differently.

___

SCENARIO 10

Child Abuse or Assault

A YOUNG CHILD is in the library with an adult, who you assume is the child's guardian. The adult is handling the child roughly, holding them tightly by their wrist and pulling them through the stacks. You approach to see if you can assist them with any library needs, and the adult brusquely declines, saying they are in a hurry and need to leave. They pick up a few books, check them out, and exit. Once they are outside the entrance, you see the adult shake the child by the shoulders and then stomp on the child's foot.

REFLECT

How does your library system suggest handling situations like these, and what training have you received? Who can you consult with at your library or externally? If you have a personal history with child abuse or trauma (or even if you don't), this experience can be very triggering. How does your own personal history impact your next steps? How might the stories you've heard about child protection come into play?

Helpful Tips

- In this scenario, the adult has behaved illegally by assaulting the child.
- As a library staff person, you may or may not be a mandatory reporter (varies by state), who is a professional bound by law to report suspected child abuse. Even if you are not mandated, you are not barred from reporting; you are just not *required* to.
- Witnessing child abuse is emotionally difficult, let alone knowing what to do about it. You should consult with local experts for guidance.
- It's hard to know how best to help keep a child safe. Thankfully, we do not have to decide, and there are experts to help. Reach out to them, and don't feel like you have to make this decision alone. Your library leadership can also help you understand what to do.

PROTECT

How can you help care for the physical safety of the child? Does the child need emergency medical services? What information can you share with local experts?

Helpful Tips

- Safety is the highest priority.
- You may call 911 to report the crime, request medical assistance, or both.
- Identify your local child-abuse reporting hotline (city, county, or state), Human Services Department, law enforcement, or other crisis-line resources.
- Once the crisis has been handled, make sure your own psychological safety is taken care of—reach out to experts to help you process and debrief your experience.

CONNECT

This scenario happened quickly, and you were not able to form a connection with the adult or child in the moment. If they return to the library, how can you support their safe library use? What supports do you need?

Helpful Tips

- You may feel compelled to try to "save" the child. Make sure your response is appropriate within the scope of your role; refer to experts that are trained for this work.
- Don't underestimate the positive impact that a friendly and respectful adult can have upon a child. By working to connect appropriately with the children at your library, you can help model what appropriate relationships look like.
- Reach out to your friends, family, and professionals to help you understand and process your feelings about stressful experiences like these.

RESPECT

In instances of abuse and assault, there often is not time for choice and collaboration with a patron. You or someone at your library will probably have had to share confidential information about the adult and child with emergency responders or local experts. However, you can respect the adult and child by keeping their other information and library use in confidence. What do your coworkers need to know about them for their work? What do they need to know to support you?

Helpful Tips

- Consider what and how much information needs to be shared, and with whom.
- Your library may have an incident report-writing system where this needs to be captured. Work with the experts at your library or with legal experts to determine the documentation requirements.
- Request supervision. This is a lot to go through, and you are not expected to do it alone.

REDIRECT

Connecting with local law enforcement and experts is key; you cannot and should not do this by yourself. Follow your library's procedure for handling emergencies and illegal behavior. If those don't exist, work with your library's leadership to create them. See how you can incorporate and highlight the strengths of your community in this work. What opportunities exist for skill-building and enhancing confidence among your staff? For your community?

Helpful Tips

- Develop and maintain relationships with social service experts. The entire community is on the same team of keeping children safe.
- Consider bringing in experts to help train staff about issues of child abuse, neglect, and reporting.

PART II • STRATEGIES AND SCENARIOS

IN PRACTICE

Share the details of a time when a similar incident occurred at your library.

_____
_____
_____
_____
_____
_____
_____
_____

How was it resolved?

_____
_____
_____
_____
_____
_____
_____
_____

Using a trauma-informed lens and the ideals of Reflect, Protect, Connect, Respect, and Redirect, consider how the incident might have concluded differently.

_____
_____
_____
_____
_____
_____
_____
_____

Solicitation or Panhandling

THERE IS A man seated outside the front entrance with a bag of belongings. Whenever a patron approaches, he gets up to talk to them and stands in front of the door before letting them pass. Several patrons have reported this behavior to staff, saying the man at the door is begging for money. Many patrons say they do not feel safe or comfortable walking by him.

REFLECT

It is likely that this patron is experiencing hardship. How has your community responded to people who solicit others for money or goods? Are there laws or rules about panhandling in your area? What are the stories you have heard about people who panhandle? What about how you "should" respond to people asking for money? What does your library say about this behavior? It may be included in your patron code of conduct.

Helpful Tips

- There is a complex interplay of individual and systemic issues at hand here. Consider that the patron who is panhandling has a depth of personal experience with hardship and financial instability, in addition to how these issues have been perpetuated throughout his lifetime.
- Be aware of your beliefs about panhandling, and how you came to them. Did your family share ideas with you? Has the media? Are they reliable sources?
- Consider connecting with a local homeless services agency to gather more information on both panhandling and the resources that are available in your area.

PROTECT

What safety issues are at play here? Where might there be opportunities to promote your patrons' physical safety? How about psychological safety? What is our responsibility as library staff?

Helpful Tips

- The other patrons trying to use the library don't feel comfortable while coming inside. There is a difference between not wanting to see someone who is experiencing poverty and feeling discomfort over this, and finding the entrance or exit physically blocked by someone else. Blocking doorways is not safe.
- Consider what policies exist about both panhandling and blocking entrances and exits. Library policies are typically grounded in ideas that promote safety by decreasing risk, or by increasing access to library services. Both are at play here.
- Remember that the patron who is panhandling has safety needs, as does every patron who uses the library.

CONNECT

How could you approach the patron who is panhandling? Consider checking in with yourself before engaging, in order to see how you are doing and what you are bringing to the encounter. It's possible this patron has had many run-ins with authority figures in the past. What can you do to ensure you have a fruitful conversation with him?

Helpful Tips

- Soften the start of the conversation. Though this may likely turn into a policy enforcement conversation, we are often better served by spending some time on relationship-building first. Share your name and ask a friendly question, such as "How are you doing today?"
- Be clear and direct. In addition to being friendly, it will be equally important to express the needs of the library. We want to kindly inform the patron of our policies related to panhandling, blocking exits, or both. Though we may assume that this patron knows what behavior we want, we are better served by sharing this information.
- Consider the relationship you have with this patron. If he is not a regular and it's his first time at the library, remember that as a community member, he is encouraged to use our spaces and resources in a safe manner. We ultimately want to serve as many people as possible, including this patron. How we interact with him today will set the tone for future engagements.

RESPECT

How can you work to show this patron respect as a library community member? What options do you have for helping him have agency or control over his experience?

Helpful Tips

- It is likely that this person has been treated unkindly in the past by other people and establishments. Treating him as an individual human being as opposed to "another panhandler" can help the interaction go smoothly.
- People who ask for money are often ignored by others. This can feel dehumanizing.
- As a community member, this patron is welcome to use the library for its resources and space. There are behaviors that are not welcome, like blocking the door and asking others for money. We want to make sure to focus on the behavior and not the person.

REDIRECT

Consider the goal of the interaction. What can you do to help work towards that goal together? Are there other needs the patron has that the library could help address?

Helpful Tips

- The ultimate goal is that this patron allows access to the building and does not solicit others for money.
- Even when we are enforcing our code of conduct or behavior expectations, there is opportunity for choice. We want to invite the patron to comply with safe behaviors; his other option is to leave the library. He is welcome to change his behavior and stay, or choose to leave. If he does neither, we can then ask other professionals and responders to come in and help.
- There may be opportunities to help link the patron to community resources, like food and clothing banks and other services that may be useful to him. You may offer to provide assistance in finding information about these services after you have explained that the panhandling and blocking access are not safe.

IN PRACTICE

Share the details of a time when a similar incident occurred at your library.

_____
_____
_____
_____
_____
_____
_____

How was it resolved?

_____
_____
_____
_____
_____
_____
_____

Using a trauma-informed lens and the ideals of Reflect, Protect, Connect, Respect, and Redirect, consider how the incident might have concluded differently.

_____
_____
_____
_____
_____
_____
_____
_____

SCENARIO 12

Stealing

A PATRON ASKS a librarian to help them find a book. The librarian helps the patron find the book and then returns to their station. The patron looks around a little more, and then the librarian notices they put the book in their bag and walk out without checking the book out.

REFLECT

Libraries are set up to provide the utmost access to information, so it can be hard for us to understand why someone would steal from the library. What would motivate this individual to steal from the library where books, movies, and other materials are already available to check out for free?

Helpful Tips

- Maybe this person was not able to get a library card. Many people struggle to provide the documentation needed to prove their address or identity, especially those experiencing homelessness.
- If they are a child or adolescent, maybe they need their parent's permission to read and check out certain books.
- Reflect on what you were taught about stealing when you were younger and how that affects your thinking on how stealing should be handled.

PROTECT

It can be difficult to navigate protecting our patrons while also protecting our library materials. A lot of times, we take pride in our materials and feel protective of our collections. However, remember that library items can be replaced. Libraries take into account that a certain number of materials will be lost, stolen, or damaged throughout the year, and these items are accounted for in the budget. If an item is stolen, treat it as you would a lost or damaged item.

Helpful Tips

- Protect your collection by advocating that more funds be set aside for replacing lost, stolen, or damaged materials.
- Protect the patron by not pursuing legal action. Most of the time, the police aren't able to track down stolen items anyway, so the incident won't be resolved through our legal system. Even with larger, more expensive items, like a computer, it is rare that these items are ever found.
- Protect yourself! Absolutely do not chase after a person or try to get the stolen items back. Your safety isn't worth any stolen item(s).

CONNECT

It is recommended to not attempt to interfere or confront the patron. However, this is not to say that you cannot connect with the individual in other ways. In retail, shoplifting prevention techniques often consist of connecting with an individual.

Helpful Tips

- Provide the staff with basic customer service skills. Even greeting patrons coming in through the door can be your first line of defense.
- It is okay to ask the patron if they need extra help or assistance. This is not accusatory, but is a way for the patron to feel connected, and it might deter stealing.

Make sure that if you do ask the patron if they need assistance, you ask several other patrons as well. That way they won't feel targeted.
- Do not confront the patron about stealing. It is not our job to accuse or to ask the patron why they stole. This puts us in a position of authority and judgment that hurts our relationship with the community.

RESPECT

As mentioned above, we want to be careful about accusing a patron of stealing. Using accusatory or judgmental language with a patron can easily escalate a situation and should be avoided.

Helpful Tips

- Refrain from using accusatory and judgmental language, such as "Did you actually check out that book?" or "Didn't you see the checkout area?"
- Remember good customer service skills: "Let me know if you need help checking out," or "I can help you over here," or even "The self-checkout is over there." Again, remember the tone and delivery of how you communicate.
- Reflecting on what a patron might be going through can help us to maintain empathy for that patron, and maintain our respect for them while interacting with them.

REDIRECT

If we reframe the way we think about stealing from the library as a victimless act, it can be easier for us to reevaluate our policies on stealing.

Helpful Tips

- Again, there is room in the budget to replace lost, damaged, or stolen items. As long as no one was hurt, book theft isn't necessarily something that needs to be brought to justice. We can simply replace these items.
- Calling the police very rarely results in a stolen item being returned anyway, so pursuing police action often isn't necessary. Though filing a police report is sometimes needed for insurance purposes, a description of the suspect is usually not required.
- You should advocate for stolen items to be treated as lost or damaged items, and include a spot in the budget for expected stolen items.

PART II • STRATEGIES AND SCENARIOS

> **IN PRACTICE**
>
> Share the details of a time when a similar incident occurred at your library.
>
> _____
> _____
> _____
> _____
> _____
> _____
> _____
>
> How was it resolved?
>
> _____
> _____
> _____
> _____
> _____
> _____
> _____
>
> Using a trauma-informed lens and the ideals of Reflect, Protect, Connect, Respect, and Redirect, consider how the incident might have concluded differently.
>
> _____
> _____
> _____
> _____
> _____
> _____
> _____
> _____

Child Unattended after Closing

AT CLOSING TIME, you see a boy who looks to be about nine years old pacing by the door. When you approach, he starts crying and says, "Please don't call the cops! Daddy will get here when he can!"

REFLECT

What might be going on with this child? He appears to have a knowledge of procedure when a child is left unattended at the library. How can you use this information to support him? What experiences might he, his family, or his community have had with police and child protection?

Helpful Tips

- This child is very upset, and may view you either as a helper or as someone who will get him "in trouble." Check in with how you are doing and try to stay calm. This will help project a sense of safety for the child.
- Imagine yourself as a child in a similar situation. What might be helpful for you to hear?
- Consider the library policies and procedures that come into play for unattended children. How can you work within those parameters while trying to promote a sense of safety?

PROTECT

The main priority is to ensure that this child is safe; therefore, leaving him outside of a closed library is not an option. If your library policy states that law enforcement or child protection must be called after a certain amount of time has passed, consider your options. You may help him call for a ride and explore safe alternatives.

Helpful Tips

- Your library and region may have rules that you must follow. Be familiar with these, so you can explain them in an age-appropriate way to the child.
- Be aware of a desire to make promises. You may feel tempted to reassure the child that you will not call the police, or that you're sure his father will get there in time. But instead, you should provide assurance of what you can do, for example, "I will stay with you while we wait for your father or the helpers to arrive."
- Driving a child patron home in your personal vehicle is not a safe option. Though you may want to, doing so may result in complicated boundary and legal concerns.

CONNECT

This child is scared. How can you approach him in a nonthreatening way? What can you do to help relieve his distress?

Helpful Tips

- Share your name with the child. This may make him more comfortable in sharing his own name and providing other information.
- Take your time. It may feel like you need to collect all the information you need upon first connecting with the child, but even a few minutes of building a relationship before getting down to business can help make the whole thing easier.
- Consider how many people need to be involved. There may be several other staff people waiting to close the library, and an audience may make his fear, anger, or embarrassment worse.

PART II • STRATEGIES AND SCENARIOS

RESPECT

Though you are dealing with a child, how can you show both him and his family respect? Consider how you talk about the situation to library staff and to any responders you may call. Trust that both the child and his family are doing their best.

Helpful Tips

- Think about what information needs to be shared, and what can be kept in confidence.
- You may be acting in the role of a trusted adult. This is an opportunity to help model safe interactions.
- Provide warm and caring support throughout your interactions. The child is upset, and your presence can help put him at ease.

REDIRECT

Consider how you can provide the child agency in his situation. If there are decisions to be made, can he help choose their order? Can he have some say in what information is shared over the phone?

Helpful Tips

- Provide some age-appropriate activity for the child while waiting. This can help serve as a distraction and keep the boy calm.
- Be aware of what choices he can participate in, and what is not appropriate. There are hard boundaries on what needs to happen (calling for help, providing certain information). Where you can provide choice for the child is in whether he talks to helpers, or if he prefers that you do. Seemingly small actions like these can help him feel more in control.

IN PRACTICE

Share the details of a time when a similar incident occurred at your library.

_____
_____
_____
_____

How was it resolved?

_____
_____
_____
_____

Using a trauma-informed lens and the ideals of Reflect, Protect, Connect, Respect, and Redirect, consider how the incident might have concluded differently.

_____
_____
_____
_____

PART III

PUTTING IT ALL TOGETHER

CONGRATULATIONS ON (ALMOST) reaching the end of the book. In this part of the book are some exercises to help you summarize what you have learned, as well as work through a few ancillary topics. In this part you are asked to reflect on what you have learned, what you plan to continue learning, and to share what you have learned with colleagues. There is the potential of great things to come for your library's patrons and community. Be inspired!

EXERCISE 1

Now It Is Your Turn

HEAD BACK TO the knowledge encapsulation exercise (activity O.1) and complete the "What I Learned" portion of it. Then, complete the following:

Goals for Myself: _____
_____
_____
_____

Steps to Take: _____
_____
_____
_____

Goals for My Library or Team: _____
_____
_____
_____

Steps to Take: _____
_____
_____
_____

Goals for My Community: _____
_____
_____
_____

Steps to Take: _____
_____
_____
_____

EXERCISE 2

Begin Anyway

AS STATED IN the introduction, this work can be hard, but it is ultimately rewarding for yourself and your community. Here are some steps that can help in moving past fear:

- Learn more.
- Practice more.
- Be prepared.
- Share with colleagues and supportive groups.
- When it gets hard, keep going.
- Work with a professional for extra support.

MOVING PAST FEAR

How can you move past fear in your own situation? How can you help colleagues to do the same? Use this space to explore some ideas.

How will I learn more? _____

How can the library support me? _____

How can the library embed self-care practices? _____

How will I practice more? _____

How will I prepare myself and library staff? _____

How can I share and discuss? What are some groups I can join or start? _____

How will I stay strong and keep going when the going gets tough? _____

EXERCISE 3

Self-Care Assessment

THE ACTIVITIES LISTED below are all things you can do to maintain your health and well-being. The goal of this assessment is to determine how well and how frequently you are performing the different self-care activities and to spotlight areas that may need a bit more attention. This list is not comprehensive, so think of it as a starting point for considering what types of self-care actions work for you.

Directions: Rate the following areas by circling the number that best relates to how well you think you are doing:
1. I do this poorly. I rarely do this.
2. Satisfactory. I do this occasionally.
3. Excellent. I am great at this!

Place a check mark next to any area (below) that you would like to work on.

PHYSICAL SELF-CARE	Poorly	Satisfactory	Excellent
☐ Eat regularly (i.e., breakfast, lunch, and dinner).	1	2	3
☐ Eat healthy foods.	1	2	3
☐ Exercise.	1	2	3
☐ Get regular medical care for prevention.	1	2	3
☐ Get regular dental care (such as cleanings).	1	2	3
☐ Get medical care when needed.	1	2	3
☐ Take time off when sick.	1	2	3
☐ Participate in fun physical activities.	1	2	3
☐ Get enough sleep.	1	2	3
☐ Take vacations.	1	2	3

PSYCHOLOGICAL SELF-CARE	Poorly	Satisfactory	Excellent
☐ Use vacation time.	1	2	3
☐ Spend time away from telephones, e-mail, and the internet.	1	2	3
☐ Make time for self-reflection.	1	2	3
☐ Write in a journal.	1	2	3
☐ Work with a professional therapist.	1	2	3
☐ Learn new things unrelated to work.	1	2	3
☐ Laugh and enjoy things that make me laugh.	1	2	3
☐ Spend time with others whose company I enjoy.	1	2	3
☐ Identify comforting activities, objects, people, and places, and then seek them out.	1	2	3
☐ Allow myself to cry.	1	2	3
☐ Express outrage in social action by protesting, petitioning, or writing a letter to the editor of a local paper.	1	2	3

SPIRITUAL SELF-CARE	Poorly	Satisfactory	Excellent
☐ Spend time reflecting or meditating.	1	2	3
☐ Spend time in nature.	1	2	3
☐ Feel inspired.	1	2	3
☐ Spend time enjoying art (such as music, film, and literature).	1	2	3
☐ Identify what is meaningful to me.	1	2	3
☐ Contribute to causes that I believe in.	1	2	3

RELATIONSHIP SELF-CARE	Poorly	Satisfactory	Excellent
☐ Schedule regular dates with my partner or spouse.	1	2	3
☐ Schedule regular activities with my children.	1	2	3
☐ Make time to see and stay in contact with friends.	1	2	3
☐ Call, check on, or see my relatives.	1	2	3
☐ Spend time with my companion animals.	1	2	3
☐ Share a fear, hope, or secret with someone I trust.	1	2	3

WORKPLACE OR PROFESSIONAL SELF-CARE	Poorly	Satisfactory	Excellent
☐ Take a break during the workday.	1	2	3
☐ Build relationships with colleagues.	1	2	3
☐ Make quiet time to complete tasks.	1	2	3
☐ Say no.	1	2	3
☐ Identify projects or tasks that are exciting and rewarding.	1	2	3
☐ Arrange workspace so it is comfortable.	1	2	3
☐ Get regular supervision.	1	2	3
☐ Advocate for myself at work.	1	2	3
☐ Work on improving my professional skills.	1	2	3
☐ Strive for balance among work, family, relationships, play, and rest.	1	2	3

Adapted from L. D. Butler, "Self-Care Assessment, University of Buffalo School of Social Work," 2010, http://socialwork.buffalo.edu/content/dam/socialwork/home/self-care-kit/self-care-assessment.pdf (originally sourced from www.ballarat.edu.au/aasp/student/sds/self_care_assess.shtml).

EXERCISE 4

Self-Care Maintenance

LOOKING AT YOUR self-care assessment, answer the following questions:

In which areas are you managing your self-care pretty well? _____
_____
_____
_____
_____

Which areas need work? _____
_____
_____
_____
_____

What is your plan to address those areas that need work? _____
_____
_____
_____
_____

What can you do to continue or start to focus on your self-care? _____
_____
_____
_____
_____

What obstacles might you encounter, and how can you overcome them? ____
_____
_____
_____
_____

EXERCISE 5

Emergency Self-Care Plan

IN THE EVENT of a rough day or a crisis, you'll want to have an emergency self-care plan in place. Complete the following prompts to put together your emergency self-care plan. You can modify this plan as you discover what works best for you. Keep it close so you can access your self-care plan as needed.

When you are upset, what can you do that will be good for you? _____

_____

_____

_____

_____

_____

Who are trusted contacts that you can reach out to? _____

_____

_____

_____

_____

_____

List some positive phrases, words, or affirmations you can say to yourself. _____

_____

_____

_____

_____

_____

What are some activities, people, and things you should avoid at this time? _____

_____

_____

_____

_____

EXERCISE 6

When Bad Things Happen

REVIEW THE COMPONENTS of an incident debriefing (see text box below) and then answer the following questions.

Does your library have a plan for debriefing after an incident? _____

What is your library's debriefing plan? Write it here: _____
_____
_____

Using information in the "Incident Debriefing" section of chapter 3, how can you improve the plan? What is missing?
_____
_____
_____

What trained facilitators can your library bring in to help debrief? _____
_____

What is the process for connecting with them (HR, manager request, etc.)?
How can you make sure that all staff are aware of the debriefing plan?
_____
_____
_____

IMPORTANT COMPONENTS OF AN INCIDENT DEBRIEFING

- Convene a meeting for those involved as soon as possible.
- Summarize the incident and address any lingering uncertainties.
- Invite questions and discuss issues of concern.
- Offer support and concern.
- Provide referrals to mental health counseling.
- Draw up a plan of action, taking into account staff needs.
- At a later time, conduct a second debrief for all staff (not just those involved).
- Answer questions and allay concerns where possible.
- Let people talk and share their perspectives.
- Offer support and referrals to mental health counseling, as needed.

EXERCISE 7

Using Your Knowledge for Justice and Change

TRY TO BRAINSTORM ways you can share the knowledge you learned in this book. Can you write an instructive article or present at a library conference? Can you train your library's staff in the techniques discussed in this book? How can what you learned move your library and your community forward?

How I will share what I learned (check one or more):
- ☐ Write an article for your library
- ☐ Create a study group with your coworkers
- ☐ Discuss what you've learned with your leadership and Board of Directors
- ☐ Ask questions
- ☐ Work with your library to include these concepts in your customer-service trainings
- ☐ Other

Be specific and elaborate on your choice(s) above.
Think about what you learned in this book. How can you use this knowledge to move your library and your community forward?

_____
_____
_____
_____
_____
_____
_____
_____
_____
_____
_____
_____
_____
_____
_____
_____
_____

EXERCISE 8

Expand Your Knowledge

LIST SOME RESOURCES and books here that you would like to explore. (You can use the end notes as a starting point and can research some additional sources.)

-
-
-
-
-
-
-
-
-
-
-
-
-
-
-
-
-
-
-
-
-
-
-
-
-
-
-

CONCLUSION
The End Is Just the Beginning

AT THE END of this workbook, we do not offer a certificate of completion that says, "Congratulations! You are now fully trauma-informed!" That certificate simply does not exist, because one can never be fully equipped to respond perfectly to each individual who has experienced adversity. Trauma's reach is too extensive and human beings are too complex for such a feat to be possible. In place of that elusive certificate and ability, by engaging with this book, you join an expanding group of library workers who are furthering their understanding of adversity and trauma in our communities. While there is no magic formula to erase every disruptive behavior you might encounter in the public library, you now have a framework for understanding how adversity may be impacting what people bring to your library. We hope that you feel empowered to respond skillfully when you see the impacts of trauma playing out at your library.

The work ahead of you is only beginning. Applying what you have learned in this workbook may take many forms. Perhaps your understanding of trauma has expanded beyond the popular conception of it as simply one-time events (as with timeline trauma); now you can look for ways that both time-limited and timeless traumas perpetuate and expose inequities that disproportionately impact marginalized communities. You may have grappled with your own experiences and realized that you, too, have a worldview and thought process that have been disrupted by trauma. Remember, experiences of adversity are not an "us versus them" or a "staff versus patrons" phenomenon. We are all at risk, and we can all engage in further healing through reflection and connection (and using professional support where needed).

Maybe you've found that a policy you have upheld does not have a "why" grounded in equity and safety. Consider talking with your supervisors and leadership to evaluate that policy. Look at your procedures that guide the staff's responses to patrons in crisis; what can you handle in the library, and when do you need to bring in other experts? We hope that the "Reflect, Protect, Connect, Respect, and Redirect" framework can help guide you in the challenging and rewarding work that is to come.

The more you apply and use the content provided by the trauma-informed lens, the more natural that perspective will become for you. We all learn from our experiences. Going forward, you can work to integrate these concepts into your library work in order to reinforce your own learning. Not unexpectedly, trauma-informed concepts are interwoven into best practices for diversity, equity, and inclusion initiatives. Trauma-informed concepts also map onto many effective de-escalation skills. There is an opportunity to use what your library is already doing as a starting place to integrate this work further. Observe what is happening at your library. What is working well?

CONCLUSION

What could be improved? What trauma-informed principles are you already using?

Another way to help solidify this learning is to have conversations with your teams and leadership. Consider sharing the book with them to see what reactions they have to the material. Perhaps you and a colleague will have identified the same common issues that occur in your library. You can work together to beef up your approaches to those issues, and afterwards discuss what worked well and what strategy to employ next time. Your colleagues know your experience at the library better than most—your team is an incredible resource for increasing your awareness and understanding.

When you do share with your team or others, be mindful of patron confidentiality. A key component of trauma-informed interaction is to help someone preserve their autonomy. This can mean helping to keep someone's story in confidence: it can take a lot for a person who has overcome adversity to disclose their private details to anyone, let alone a helping professional. Consider what details or information can be shared safely with your teammates, and what might be better left unsaid. A patron who tells one library staff member about their life may feel re-traumatized to learn that the information was shared with other staff members. It is an honor to engage with another human being about their life, whether through a community resource request or a disclosure about a book they enjoyed. Instead of saying, "Hey, everyone! Frank told me he had a mental health crisis that caused him to lose his housing," you can share that a patron confided in you about their mental health and housing concerns. Consider following up by asking your colleagues for resources or ideas for the patron. You can also absolutely ask for coworkers to help you understand how hard it is to see a patron go through something like this. Engaging with patrons who are experiencing life challenges is hard work; test yourself to see if you can get the support you need to be an effective helper without sharing details told in confidence. Trauma and adversity impact us all, and helping to preserve confidentiality where and when we can is one way we can all work together to help each other heal.

There will be times when you and your teams need to look outside the library for additional coaching and learning on these topics. We encourage you to work with experts in your community to continue learning more. Most community mental health centers are happy to partner with libraries, and help work with their staff on best approaches for engaging with patrons who have experienced adversity. Because so much of this material is rooted deeply in human interactions, it can be very useful to bring in professionals and peer counselors who have lived experience to discuss this important work.

Webinars and trainings on trauma are becoming more available as the extent of adversity in our communities has been exposed. When you seek out additional learning on this topic, try to critically evaluate those information sources that declare they are authorities on serving populations who regularly experience hardship, like homelessness. Do the materials they put out use trauma-informed concepts? Do they, for example, recognize that people experiencing life challenges are in fact human beings, and try to avoid using language labels like "addicts," "homeless," or "mentally ill"? Does their work point to an understanding of how systems are designed to perpetuate disparities through race, gender, ability status, and any of the other identities that correlate highly with experiences of adversity? Do they focus on the behavior being challenging rather than on the individuals themselves being difficult? We know that trauma affects our brains, and often this is observable through our behaviors. Our experiences do not define us; be wary of "experts" who suggest that they do.

And when we in libraries find ourselves on the front lines of community adversity, the temptation to reach out to those who are selling a "quick fix" is understandable. When helpers are exposed to trauma regularly without the appropriate education and supervision to deal with it, they may experience a host of reactions, including feeling hopeless or helpless; feeling that they cannot do enough to help; difficulty appreciating nuance or complexity; anger, fear, and guilt; or experiencing an inflated sense of importance in their work. These are uncomfortable experiences, and when we're trying to cope with them, to be told that there's a host of learning and a lifetime of work ahead of us is not what most people are hoping to hear. However, this hard work is in line with the mission of the public library: to provide essential resources to everyone in our community. The quick fixes can push the most vulnerable people away, when we want to do the opposite to have a healing and healthy community.

To be effective on our journey of applying a trauma-informed lens, there is some work we need to undertake on ourselves. Coming to terms with our own history of adversity is a big step that often requires time, connection with others, and sometimes professional guidance. We may need to frequently check in with ourselves about the motivations that drive our library work: *Why do I choose to do this work? In what ways am I called to serve the community?*

And outside of ourselves and our own motivations, we are impacted by our teams and library culture. Determine who among your colleagues you can confide in about this work. Notice the energy and influence they have. Seek out mentors who can guide you in hope and integrity. Additionally, make sure to care for yourself within the structure of your work. Take breaks. Utilize the sick leave and vacation time that you are entitled to. These necessities have been fought for because the labor movement acutely understands that human beings require time to breathe, to relax, and to heal.

There is no one-size-fits-all approach to how you can best undertake your library work with a trauma-informed lens. This workbook is a starting point that offers many ideas and several approaches. You are in charge of your journey from here, and the work will be alternately joyful and painful, numbing and exhilarating, and often, all of this at once. But by setting out to engage with this mindset, you are engaging in an overwhelmingly hopeful act—the belief that people can heal and grow from what they have endured, and that the library is a place where healing can begin.

ABOUT THE PRINCIPAL WRITER AND ADVISOR AND THE CONTRIBUTORS

DEBRA WALSH KEANE, LCSW, came to library social work from a clinical background in community mental health. She was the first social worker employed by the Jefferson County (CO) Public Library. She is honored to have collaborated on this book and hopes it will be a tool for growth and healing in library communities.

Jean Badalamenti, MSW, is the DC Public Library's health and human services assistant manager, working in the service design and engagement office.

Leah Esguerra is a California licensed marriage and family therapist (LMFT). She manages the San Francisco Public Library's Social Service Program. Leah served as one of the cochairs of the Public Library Association's Social Worker Task Force until 2020.

Melissa Glenn is a licensed mental health counselor in Washington State. She has several years of experience providing therapeutic services in clinical and educational settings. She also has trained library staff across the country. Melissa brings a whole health, trauma-informed perspective to mental health and community work.

Elissa Hardy, LCSW, has worked in the social work field for twenty years. She focuses on the realm of homelessness and also teaches master's-level social work students. She has worked at the Denver Public Library for the past six years.

Kathleen Hughes is the editor of *Public Libraries* magazine and the manager of publications, Public Library Association.

Sarah C. Johnson, MLIS, LMSW, is an assistant professor and social sciences librarian at Hunter College Libraries (City University of New York). She researches, writes, and instructs on the intersection of social work and public libraries.

Margaret Ann Paauw is a licensed clinical social worker who practices library social work at the Chicago Public Library. She is currently working on her PhD in social work from Loyola University Chicago, with a dissertation topic on library social work programs across the United States.

ABOUT THE PRINCIPAL WRITER AND ADVISOR AND THE CONTRIBUTORS

Lee Patterson is the social work director at the Richland (SC) Public Library.

David Perez is the social work and diversity services manager at the Long Branch (NJ) Public Library.

Ruby Rivera, LICSW, is the library social worker for the Saint Paul (MN) Public Libraries. She works with diverse populations in multiple settings, including substance abuse, education, and the social service field. She has eighteen years of experience in serving families, adults, and children.

Tiffany Russell, LMSW, is a licensed clinical social worker. She has been in the social work field for seventeen years. Tiffany has experience in community mental health and in the emerging field of library social work.

Susan Voss-Rothmeier has been the social worker in the Multnomah County Libraries in Portland, Oregon, since the program's inception in 2016. She is a licensed clinical social worker with more than twenty-three years' experience in the fields of mental health crisis and homelessness.

INDEX

A

abuse
    adult self-neglect scenario, 57
    child abuse or assault scenario, 60–62
    trauma from, 3–4
access, 13
ACE (Adverse Childhood Experiences) study, 8–9
ACE questionnaire, 8, 9
activities
    Considering Patron Behavior, 12
    Identifying Resource Gaps, 17
    Knowledge Encapsulation chart, xii–xiii
    Library Policies Review, 14
    Other Words, 22
    Resource Referral Practice, 29
    Setting Boundaries Practice, 29
adult self-neglect scenario, 57–59
Adverse Childhood Experiences (ACE) study, 8–9
adversity
    ACE questionnaire, 8–9
    as "all of us" issue, 8
    history of, coming to terms with, 83
    relationships for healing from, 7
    training about, 82
    trauma and, 3, 4, 81
alcohol
    substance use scenario, 48–50
    suspected intoxication, under the influence scenario, 45–47
anger, 34
assault, 60–62
assessment
    reference interview questions, 16
    self-care assessment, 30
    ten steps to building skills, 32
assumptions, 11, 39
at-risk adults, 57–59

B

Badalamenti, Jean, 85
ban, 23
barriers, 24
Begin Anyway exercise, 73
behavior expectations
    informing patrons of, 20, 43
    panhandling patron and, 64
    in substance use scenario, 49
    suspension of library privileges and, 24
    threatening verbal/nonverbal behavior scenario, 52
behaviors
    adult self-neglect scenario, 57–59
    broken rules, brain changes with, 4
    challenging behaviors of patrons, xi, 11–14
    child abuse or assault scenario, 60–62
    Considering Patron Behavior activity, 12
    de-escalation, 19–20
    emergency services, contacting, 21
    in mental health challenge scenario, 34
    personal belongings scenario, 42–44
    rational detachment and, 30
    sleeping at library scenario, 36–38
    solicitation or panhandling scenario, 63–65
    stealing scenario, 66–68
    strong personal odor scenario, 39–41
    substance use scenario, 48–50
    suspected intoxication, under the influence scenario, 45–47
    suspension of library privileges and, 23–24
    threatening verbal/nonverbal behavior scenario, 51–53
    trauma-informed lens on, 5–7
belongings
    of patrons, awareness of, 46
    personal belongings scenario, 42–44
    of unsheltered teens, 54

INDEX

bias
  about patron with strong personal odor, 39
  awareness of, 6
  library policies, enforcement of, 13
  in personal belongings scenario, 42
  in policing, 23
  in suspected intoxication, under the influence scenario, 45
  against threatening behavior, 51
  against unsheltered teens, 54
Black, Indigenous, and People of Color (BIPOC), 3
body language
  in mental health challenge scenario, 33, 34
  nonverbals, 20–21
  patron with strong personal odor and, 40
body odor, 39–41
boundaries
  guidelines for maintaining, 26–27
  Setting Boundaries Practice activity, 29
  for sharing of personal information, 28
brain
  broken rules and, 4
  changes from trauma, 4–5
  trauma's effect on, 82
budget, 66, 67
burnout, 25, 27, 30

C

"cars stop at stop signs" rule, 4–5
cell phone, 33, 48
challenges, 32
challenging behavior
  Considering Patron Behavior activity, 12
  factors to consider, 11
  library policies, 11, 13
  Library Policies Review activity, 14
Chambers of Commerce, 18
child abuse or assault scenario, 60–62
child protection, 69
child unattended after closing scenario, 69–70
child-abuse reporting hotline, 60
childhood, ACE questionnaire about, 8–9
children
  child abuse or assault scenario, 60–62
  child unattended after closing scenario, 69–70
  library policies, enforcement of, 13
  new rules created by trauma, 5
  stealing from library, 66
  suspension of library privileges, 24
choice
  in adult self-neglect scenario, 58
  enforcement of library policies through, 20
  for patron under the influence, 46–47
  respect of patron's choice, 43
  Respect strategies for, 7–8
  self-determination and, 8
  for unattended child at library, 70
CITs (crisis intervention teams), 23
clothing, 40, 57
coaching, 82
collaboration, 7–8
comfort zone, 32
communication
  in adult self-neglect scenario, 57–58
  emergency services and, 23
  in mental health challenge scenario, 33
  In Other Words activity, 22
  with panhandling patron, 63–64
  with patron with strong personal odor, 40
  in personal belongings scenario, 43
  stealing by patron and, 67
  in substance use scenario, 49
  in suspected intoxication, under the influence scenario, 46
  suspension of library privileges and, 23–24
  in threatening verbal/nonverbal behavior scenario, 51–52
  verbals, 21
community mental health centers, 82
computers, 51–53
confidence, 8
confidentiality
  child abuse or assault and, 61
  of patron, mindfulness of, 82
  of patron, social services referral and, 27–28
  suspected intoxication, under the influence scenario, 45
  of unattended child at library, 70
  See also privacy
Connect strategies
  for adult self-neglect, 57–58
  for child abuse or assault, 60–61

for child unattended after closing, 69
function of, 31
for mental health challenges, 33
for personal belongings, 42–43
relationships, focus on, 7
for sleeping at the library, 36–37
for solicitation or panhandling, 63–64
for stealing, 66–67
for strong personal odor, 40
for substance use, 49
for suspected intoxication, under the influence, 46
for threatening verbal/nonverbal behavior, 51
for unsheltered teens, 54–55
Considering Patron Behavior activity, 12
cortisol, 4
county websites, 18
crisis, 19–20
crisis intervention teams (CITs), 23
crisis lines, 18
cultural issues, 6
customer service skills, 66–67

D

databases, resource, 18
debriefing
    after child abuse/assault incident, 60
    benefits of, 25
    considerations for implementing, 25–26
    definition of, 24
    follow-up to, 26
    of library staff, 15
    questions for, 26
    When Bad Things Happen exercise, 78
decision-making
    in adult self-neglect scenario, 58
    enforcement of library policies through choice, 20
    self-determination and, 8
    shared, opportunities for, 7
    See also choice
de-escalation
    choice for, 20
    kindly inform, 20
    nonverbals for, 20–21
    pre-escalation work, 19–20
    threatening verbal/nonverbal behavior scenario, 51–53
    verbals for, 21
documentation, 66
driver's license, 19
drugs
    substance use scenario, 48–50
    suspected intoxication, under the influence scenario, 45–47

E

Emergency Self-Care Plan, 77
emergency services
    contacting about child abuse/assault, 60, 61
    decision about contacting, 21, 23
    for patron using substances, 48
    questions about how/when to involve, 15
    sleeping guidance from, 36
    in substance use scenario, 48, 49
    for trespassing cases, 24
emotions, 4, 73
empathy, 34, 39, 67
environment
    See space
equity, 13
escalation, 11, 21
    See also de-escalation
Esguerra, Leah, 85
exercises
    Begin Anyway, 73
    Emergency Self-Care Plan, 77
    Expand Your Knowledge, 80
    Now It Is Your Turn, 72
    for self-care, 28, 30
    Self-Care Assessment, 74–75
    Self-Care Maintenance, 76
    Using Your Knowledge for Justice and Change, 79
    When Bad Things Happen, 78
Expand Your Knowledge exercise, 80
expectations
    See behavior expectations
eye contact, 20, 33

F

facilitator, 25, 26
fear, 73
feedback, 7, 8
"fight, flight, or freeze" responses, 5, 11

INDEX

follow-up, to debriefing, 26
food, 28, 30
framework, trauma-informed lens, xi, 5–8

G
Glenn, Melissa, 85
goals, 32, 64, 72
government, 18, 19

H
hallucination, 34
Hardy, Elissa, 85
harm reduction, 48
Harris, Nadine Burke, 5
health, 45–47
    See also self-care
historical issues, 6
homeless people
    choices of, library staff and, 8
    ID for access to services and, 19
    personal belongings scenario, 42–44
    sleeping at the library scenario, 36–38
    solicitation or panhandling scenario, 63–65
    strong personal odor scenario, 39–41
    trauma experienced by, 3–4
    unsheltered teens scenario, 54–56
homeless services agency, 63
housing/shelter, 37, 54–56
Hughes, Kathleen, 85
Human Resources, 24, 25
Human Services Department, 60
hygiene, 39–41, 57–59
hyper-arousal, 5

I
ID, 19
Identifying Resource Gaps activity, 17
In Practice worksheet
    for adult self-neglect scenario, 59
    for child abuse or assault scenario, 62
    for mental health challenges scenario, 35
    for patron with strong personal odor scenario, 41
    for personal belongings scenario, 44
    for sleeping at the library, 38
    for solicitation or panhandling scenario, 65
    for stealing scenario, 68
    for substance use scenario, 50
    for suspected intoxication, under the influence scenario, 47
    for threatening verbal/nonverbal behavior scenario, 53
    for unattended child at library scenario, 70
    for unsheltered teens scenario, 56
incident debriefing, 24–26, 78
information
    communication of, 34
    sources for patrons, 16, 18

J
Johnson, Sarah C., 85
judgment, 40, 49, 67

K
Keane, Debra Walsh, 85
knowledge
    Expand Your Knowledge exercise, 80
    Knowledge Encapsulation chart, xii–xiii
    Now It Is Your Turn exercise, 72
    Using Your Knowledge for Justice and Change exercise, 79

L
language
    guidance on, 21
    for mental health challenges, 33
    In Other Words activity, 22
    patron sleeping at library and, 37
    See also communication
law enforcement, 60, 61
    See also emergency services; police
learning, 32
LGBTQ community, 42
library
    incident debriefing, 24–26
    library privileges, suspending, 15, 23–24
    self-care, support of, 28
    sleeping at the library scenario, 36–38
    trauma experiences in, xiv
    trauma-informed lens of, 5
    trauma-informed work, guidance on, 81–83

INDEX

library patrons
- adult self-neglect scenario, 57–59
- boundaries of library staff and, 26–27
- challenging behaviors of, xi, 11–14
- child abuse or assault scenario, 60–62
- child unattended after closing scenario, 69–70
- confidentiality for, 27–28, 82
- Considering Patron Behavior activity, 12
- debriefing, 26
- de-escalation work, 19–20
- emergency services, contacting, 21, 23
- "fight, flight, or freeze" behaviors, 5
- library privileges, suspending, 23–24
- mental health challenges scenario, 33–35
- needs of, xiv
- nonverbals and, 20–21
- personal belongings scenario, 42–44
- relationships with, 7
- resource navigation/referrals/reference interview, 15–16
- search tips, 18–19
- sleeping at the library scenario, 36–38
- solicitation or panhandling scenario, 63–65
- stealing scenario, 66–68
- strong personal odor scenario, 39–41
- substance use scenario, 48–50
- suspected intoxication, under the influence scenario, 45–47
- threatening verbal/nonverbal behavior scenario, 51–53
- trauma-informed lens for library staff, 5–8
- trauma-informed principles for working with, 15
- unsheltered teens scenario, 54–56

library policies
- about sleeping at library, 36, 37
- about substance use in library, 48
- challenging behavior and, 11, 13
- consideration of, 81
- de-escalation and, 20
- patron choice and, 8
- on solicitation or panhandling, 63
- on unattended children, 69

Library Policies Review activity, 14
library social workers, 15, 16
library staff
- adult self-neglect scenario, 57–59
- Begin Anyway exercise, 73
- boundaries, maintaining, 26–27
- challenging behavior, navigating, 11–14
- child abuse or assault scenario, 60–62
- child unattended after closing scenario, 69–70
- de-escalation by, 19–20
- Emergency Self-Care Plan exercise, 77
- emergency services, contacting, 21, 23
- Expand Your Knowledge exercise, 80
- "fight, flight, or freeze" behaviors and, 5
- Identifying Resource Gaps activity, 17
- incident debriefing, 24–26
- information sources for patrons, 16, 18
- Knowledge Encapsulation chart, xii–xiii
- library privileges, suspending, 23–24
- mental health challenges scenario, 33–35
- nonverbal presentation of, 20–21
- Now It Is Your Turn exercise, 72
- In Other Words activity, 22
- personal belongings scenario, 42–44
- resource navigation, referral, reference interview, 15–16
- search tips, 18–19
- Self-Care Assessment exercise, 74–75
- self-care by, xiv, 28–30
- Self-Care Maintenance exercise, 76
- sleeping at the library scenario, 36–38
- solicitation or panhandling scenario, 63–65
- stealing scenario, 66–68
- strong personal odor scenario, 39–41
- substance use scenario, 48–50
- suspected intoxication, under the influence scenario, 45–47
- threatening verbal/nonverbal behavior scenario, 51–53
- trauma, working with, xiv
- trauma-informed lens, xi, 5–8, 82
- trauma-informed work of, 81–83
- unsheltered teens scenario, 54–56
- Using Your Knowledge for Justice and Change exercise, 79
- When Bad Things Happen exercise, 78

limitations, 27
local government, 18
local resource guides, 18

INDEX

M
mediation, 24–26
medications, 36
mental health, 23
mental health challenges scenario, 33–35
mentors, 83
middle-class norms, 6, 13
misunderstandings, 20
money, 63–65

N
Narcan, 48
needs, 19, 28
"no" statement, 27
"No Talking!" stereotype, 11
nonverbal behavior, 20–21, 51–53
norms, 6, 13
Now It Is Your Turn exercise, 72

O
odor, strong personal odor scenario, 39–41
older adults, 57–59
open-ended questions, 16
Other Words activity, 22

P
Paauw, Margaret Ann, 85
panhandling, 63–65
patrons
    See library patrons
Patterson, Lee, 86
Perez, David, 86
personal belongings scenario, 42–44
personal information, 27–28
plan, self-care, 30
police
    child unattended after closing scenario, 69
    contacting about child abuse/assault, 60
    decision about contacting, 21, 23
    questions about how/when to involve, 15
    safety at library and, 6
    stealing by patron and, 66, 67
policies
    See library policies
power, 7, 43
practice, 32

pre-escalation work, 19–20
priorities, 19
privacy
    in adult self-neglect scenario, 58
    of patron, 45, 82
    social services referral and, 27–28
    of unsheltered teens, 55
    See also confidentiality
Protect strategies
    for adult self-neglect, 57
    for child abuse or assault, 60
    for child unattended after closing, 69
    function of, 31
    for mental health challenges, 33–34
    for personal belongings, 42
    for safety, 6–7
    for sleeping at the library, 36
    for solicitation or panhandling, 63
    for stealing, 66
    for strong personal odor, 39
    for substance use, 48–49
    for suspected intoxication, under the influence, 45–46
    for threatening verbal/nonverbal behavior, 51
    for unsheltered teens, 54
public library
    trauma-informed lens, 5–8
    working with people at, xiv
    See also library

Q
questions
    for debriefing, 26
    open-ended, 16
    for reference interview, 16
    in substance use scenario, 49

R
racism, 13
rational detachment, 30
Redirect strategies
    for adult self-neglect, 58
    for child abuse or assault, 61
    for child unattended after closing, 70
    function of, 31
    for mental health challenges, 34

INDEX

for personal belongings, 43
for skill-building/confidence, 8
for sleeping at the library, 37
for solicitation or panhandling, 64
for stealing, 67
for strong personal odor, 40
for substance use, 49
for suspected intoxication, under the influence, 46–47
for threatening verbal/nonverbal behavior, 52
for unsheltered teens, 55
reference interview
    questions for, 16
    relationships, focus on, 7
    Resource Referral Practice activity, 29
    trauma-informed approaches for, 15
referral
    in adult self-neglect scenario, 58
    confidentiality of patron and, 27–28
    help from library staff with, 15–16
    resource navigation search tips, 18–19
    Resource Referral Practice activity, 29
    resources, where to search, 16, 18
Reflect, Protect, Connect, Respect, and *Redirect*
  framework
    as guide, 81
    overview of, 31
    strategies of, 5–8
Reflect strategies
    for adult self-neglect, 57
    for child abuse or assault, 60
    for child unattended after closing, 69
    cultural/historical issues, consideration of, 6
    function of, 31
    for mental health challenges, 33
    for personal belongings, 42
    for sleeping at the library, 36
    for solicitation or panhandling, 63
    for stealing, 66
    for strong personal odor, 39
    for substance use, 48
    for suspected intoxication, under the influence, 45
    for threatening verbal/nonverbal behavior, 51
    for unsheltered teens, 54
reinstatement process, 24
relationships
    in adult self-neglect scenario, 57–58
    connection with children, 61
    for mental health challenges, 33
    with panhandling patron, 64
    patron sleeping at the library and, 37
    with patrons, 7, 11
    in personal belongings scenario, 42–43
    with unattended child at library, 69–70
reporting, 60–61
resilience, 3, 5, 27, 30
resource databases, 18
resource navigation
    help from library staff with, 15–16
    search tips, 18–19
resource referral
    See referral
Resource Referral Practice activity, 29
resources
    Expand Your Knowledge exercise, 80
    Identifying Resource Gaps activity, 17
    information sources for patrons, 16, 18
    for panhandling patron, 64
    for patron using substances, 49
    for patron with strong personal odor, 40
    for patron with suspected intoxication, 46
    reference interview questions, 16
    Resource Referral Practice activity, 29
    for unsheltered teens, 55
respect, 39, 40, 49
Respect strategies
    for adult self-neglect, 58
    for child abuse or assault, 61
    for child unattended after closing, 70
    choice/collaboration, engagement in, 7–8
    function of, 31
    for mental health challenges, 33
    for personal belongings, 43
    for sleeping at the library, 37
    for solicitation or panhandling, 64
    for stealing, 67
    for strong personal odor, 40
    for substance use, 49
    for suspected intoxication, under the influence, 46
    for threatening verbal/nonverbal behavior, 52
    for unsheltered teens, 55
risk, 13

INDEX

Rivera, Ruby, 86
rules, 4–5
    See also library policies
Russell, Tiffany, 86

S

safety
    in adult self-neglect scenario, 57
    child abuse or assault scenario, 60–61
    child unattended after closing scenario, 69–70
    library policies for, 13
    library privileges and, 23
    mental health challenges and, 33–34
    patron with strong personal odor and, 39
    in personal belongings scenario, 42
    Protect strategies for, 6–7
    sleeping at the library scenario, 36
    solicitation or panhandling scenario, 63
    stealing from library and, 66
    substance use scenario, 48–49
    in suspected intoxication, under the influence scenario, 45–46
    threatening verbal/nonverbal behavior scenario, 51
    for unsheltered teens, 54
scenarios
    adult self-neglect, 57–59
    child abuse or assault, 60–62
    child unattended after closing, 69–70
    mental health challenges, 33–35
    personal belongings, 42–44
    sleeping at the library, 36–38
    solicitation or panhandling, 63–65
    stealing, 66–68
    strong personal odor, 39–41
    substance use, 48–50
    suspected intoxication, under the influence, 45–47
    threatening verbal/nonverbal behavior, 51–53
    tools for, 31
    unsheltered teens, 54–56
schedule, 25
search
    information sources for patrons, 16, 18
    tips for, 18–19
self-awareness, 45

self-care
    after mental health challenge, 35
    description of, 28
    Emergency Self-Care Plan exercise, 77
    final guidance on, 83
    by library staff, xiv
    self-care assessment, 30
    Self-Care Assessment exercise, 74–75
    Self-Care Maintenance exercise, 76
    self-care plan, 30
    suggestions for, 28, 30
self-neglect, 57–59
skills
    scenarios/tools for practicing, 31
    skill-building of library patrons, 8
    ten steps to building, 32
sleep deprivation, 36
sleeping at the library scenario, 36–38
smiling, 20
social services
    boundaries of library staff and, 26–27
    confidentiality of patron and, 27–28
    debriefing, leader of, 25
    relationships with, 61
    resource navigation search tips, 18–19
    resources for, 18
    resources for unsheltered teens, 54, 55
solicitation or panhandling scenario, 63–65
space
    comfortable workspace, 30
    for debriefing, 25
    between patron and staff, 21
speech
    guidance on, 21
    In Other Words activity, 22
    words for waking someone up, 37
    See also communication
staff
    See library staff
state ID, 19
stealing scenario, 66–68
stereotypes, 6, 11
strategies, 31
stress hormones, 4–5
strong personal odor scenario, 39–41
substance use scenario, 48–50

INDEX

support, 28
suspected intoxication, under the influence scenario, 45–47
suspension, of library privileges, 23–24

T

teenagers, unsheltered teens scenario, 54–56
theft, 66–68
threat, 11
threatening verbal/nonverbal behavior scenario, 51–53
time, 25
"timeless" trauma, 3
"time-limited" trauma, 3
"timeline" trauma, 3
tools/techniques
    boundaries, 26–27
    confidentiality, 27–28
    de-escalation in trauma-informed environment, 19–20
    emergency services, 21, 23
    Identifying Resource Gaps activity, 17
    incident debriefing, 24–26
    information sources for patrons, 16, 18
    library privileges, suspending, 23–24
    nonverbals, 20–21
    In Other Words activity, 22
    Reflect, Protect, Connect, Respect, and *Redirect* tools, 31
    resource navigation, referral, reference interview, 15–16
    Resource Referral Practice activity, 29
    search tips, 18–19
    self-care, 28, 30
    trauma-informed principles, 15
    verbals, 21
touching, 36, 37, 51
training, 82
trans and gender-diverse individuals, 3
transition ritual, 30
trauma
    Adverse Childhood Experiences study, 8–9
    brain chemistry changes from, 4–5
    challenging behaviors of library patrons and, xi
    conclusion about, 81–83
    definition of, 3
    impact on people, xiv

    trauma-informed, meaning of, 5–8
Trauma Informed Care Project, 31
trauma-informed lens
    conclusion about, 81–83
    Connect strategies, 7
    de-escalation in trauma-informed environment, 19–20
    framework to use, xi
    library's use of, 5
    meaning of, 5–6
    In Other Words activity, 22
    Promote strategies, 6–7
    Redirect strategies, 8
    Reflect strategies, 6
    Respect strategies, 7–8
    verbal communication and, 21
trauma-informed principles
    scenarios/tools for incorporating, 31
    use of, 81–82
    for working with library patrons, 15
traumatic experiences, 24–26
trespassing, 24
trust, 7, 25

U

unsheltered teens scenario, 54–56
Using Your Knowledge for Justice and Change exercise, 79

V

verbal behavior, 21, 51–53
Voss-Rothmeier, Susan, 86

W

webinars, 82
websites, 18
well-being
    Self-Care Assessment exercise, 74–75
    self-care for, 28
    Self-Care Maintenance exercise, 76
    self-care plan for, 30
When Bad Things Happen exercise, 78
whiteness, 6
Wi-Fi, 33–35
women, 3
workspace, 30